# BUILDING RESILIENT ORGANIZATIONS

BEST PRACTICES, TOOLS, AND INSIGHTS TO THRIVE
IN EVER-CHANGING CONTEXTS

**www.pmi.org**
**www.brightline.org**
**www.thinkers50.com**

First published in the USA 2022

**ISBN:**
978-1-62825-779-3 (Paperback)
978-1-62825-780-9 (eBook)

**Published by:**
Project Management Institute, Inc.
14 Campus Boulevard
Newtown Square, Pennsylvania 19073-3299 USA
Phone: +1 610 356 4600
Fax: +1 610 356 4647
Email: customercare@pmi.org
Internet: www.PMI.org

**Design by www.jebensdesign.co.uk**

## Library of Congress Cataloging-in-Publication Data

Names: Project Management Institute, publisher. | Brightline Initiative, issuer.

Title: Building resilient organizations : best practices, tools, and insights to thrive in ever-changing contexts / Project Management Institute, Inc., Brightline Initiative.

Description: Newtown Square, Pennsylvania : Project Management Institute, Inc., 2022. | Includes bibliographical references. | Summary: "In our tumultuous times, understanding and achieving resilience have never been more important. Some organizations have resilience in their DNA. They possess the agility of mind, culture, and organization to survive and thrive no matter what is put in their way. Building Resilient Organizations is focused on identifying what sets these enterprises apart, exploring the nature of resilience for organizations. Along the way, we discover some inspiring global examples of resilient projects in practice and some novel thinking for leaders to consider about what it takes to be resilient over the long haul. With contributions from leading thinkers and practitioners from throughout the world, Building Resilient Organizations will enable you and your organization to further develop resilience as a muscle in your organization"-- Provided by publisher.

Identifiers: LCCN 2022044027 (print) | LCCN 2022044028 (ebook) | ISBN 9781628257793 (paperback) | ISBN 9781628257809 (ebook)

Subjects: LCSH: Organizational change. | Business planning. | Project management. | BISAC: BUSINESS & ECONOMICS / Project Management

Classification: LCC HD58.8 .B85 2022 (print) | LCC HD58.8 (ebook) | DDC 658.4/063--dc23/eng/20231031

LC record available at https://lccn.loc.gov/2022044027

LC ebook record available at https://lccn.loc.gov/2022044028

# Contents

# Foreword

Next time you are walking through a shopping mall or down Main Street in a town most anywhere in the world, look around at the names above the stores. Then cast your mind back to the names you saw over those stores 10, 20, 30 years ago. It can be virtually guaranteed that more than 90% of the names above those storefronts will be different.

It is not just in the world of retail that we see massive turnover of names, brands, and companies. A vast body of research examining corporate longevity suggests that companies come and go, their fortunes wax and wane. Only a select few demonstrate real staying power. This is a fact of corporate life. But for many organizations, it need not be that way. They can embrace change, technology, and innovation. They can prioritize their customers and employees and create an organizational culture where change and transformation are integral pieces of their corporate DNA.

As we have seen amidst the challenges of the past several years, some organizations intrinsically have this sort of resilience in their DNA. *Building Resilient Organizations* is focused on identifying what sets these enterprises apart, exploring the nature of resilience for organizations and how organizations can follow suit to harness the power of transformation to excel against the challenges of tomorrow. Along the way, we discover some inspiring global examples of resilient projects in practice and some novel thinking for leaders to consider what is really needed to be a resilient organization.

None of this is easy. But, in the ever-evolving world of work, understanding and achieving resilience has never been more important. We hope that *Building Resilient Organizations* will enable you to embed transformation and resilience into your organization.

**Pierre Le Manh**
President and CEO, Project Management Institute

# Organizational Resilience Through Culture

EMIL ANDERSSON AND
TAHIROU ASSANE OUMAROU

1

Academic research identifies three main streams of thought in how we understand the notion of resilience:

1. something an organization *has*,
2. something an organization *does*, and
3. a measure of disturbances that an organization can *tolerate*.

This research concludes: "Resilience, at the organizational level, is the measurable combination of characteristics, abilities, capacities or capabilities that allows an organization to withstand known and unknown disturbances and still survive." (Ruiz-Martin, 2018, p. 21). Given this description, it is little wonder that resilience is a much-repeated phrase—and aspiration—for organizational leaders throughout the world.

The assumption commonly made is that organizational resilience is an issue of our time. The evidence for this is undoubtedly very strong. The presence of a volatile, uncertain, complex, and ambiguous (VUCA) environment fundamentally challenges the way we organize and work. Daily, we witness the speed of change resulting from intensified competition, changing sociopolitical landscapes, altered customer expectations, and technological advancements. It is daunting for organizations to develop strategies and organizational capabilities that simply work under these conditions and the current state of turmoil. Instead, organizations need to sense and respond to change a great deal more in today's business environment. Adaptation to external conditions is therefore a crucial aspect of business. This is a form of organizational sensitivity—an ability to move fast as the situation evolves and as multilayered global contexts shift. The ability to meet these conditions starts from within the organization.

While these are unprecedented times, we are not alone in experiencing turbulence and technological leaps. Companies have been responding to crises and the unexpected since their very inception. Consider what happened during World War II when companies changed their entire product lines to support the war effort. In the United States, Cadillac and Chrysler manufactured tanks, Oldsmobile made heavy caliber shells, Packard made boat engines, and IBM expanded its product line to include Browning automatic rifles. In Japan, Matsushita produced ships and planes with no experience in either product (Crainer, 2000).

The organizational ability to survive and thrive in unpredictable conditions has long been a source of research and, for those on the organizational front line, worry. Now, in the wake of COVID-19, there is an opportunity to understand more about organizational resilience. There are many cases of companies surviving the last three years against the odds and seizing the opportunity to adapt. Bill Fischer of the International Institute for Management and Development (IMD) reports on a brilliant example of adaption: the story of Gong Yi, the R&D director of a microenterprise within the Chinese white-goods company Haier (Fischer, 2021). Waiting at a vaccination center, he noted a Haier refrigerator. In a busy clinic, the door of the refrigerator was hardly ever closed; he realized this compromised the condition of the vaccines, which needed to be stored at a constant temperature. Along with two colleagues, Gong Yi set out to develop a new refrigerator with eight doors. The team then gave themselves the task of changing the entire vaccination customer experience in China's 52,000 vaccination centers; they now offer turnkey renovations of centers along with the custom-developed refrigerators.

Such stories—and there are many worldwide in the wake of the pandemic—offer hope and suggest resilience is largely a matter of turning challenges into opportunities. This opportunistic element is important, but the key realization of the last few years is that building organizational resiliency is a long and deliberate process rather than a one-time occurrence. While a crisis can make the need and value more apparent, preparatory actions must be taken, even without a crisis.

Resilience, in turn, reflects an organization's culture. The power of people and culture can often be held back by inefficient organizational hierarchies and silos, as well as differences in basic assumptions. In turn, a poor organizational culture contributes to fragmentation and anxiety among employees, all of which lower the chances of becoming resilient (Brightline Initiative, 2019).

In the case of Gong Yi, the key facilitation for his strategic insight was the fact that Haier has a culture built around microenterprises. It has a lengthy track record of actively encouraging employees to come up with ideas and develop them into stand-alone businesses. Strategic insight plus culture is a potent combination.

Our work at Brightline® suggests that resilient cultures have the following four vital elements:

### Culture Through Leadership

As indicated by the much-acclaimed expert on culture and leadership, Ed Schein, culture is fundamentally anchored and dependent on the actions of the organization's leadership. To change the culture, it is crucial to have leaders who collectively and convincingly communicate the needed change and inspiringly model the new target behaviors (Brightline Initiative, 2018).

The challenge for leaders is to create conditions so that others feel capable and safe to step forward, and recognize that not everyone will want or need to lead a team. Leaders need followers to be successful and so they need to make *followership* a valued behavior. Rather than always looking for ways to lead, good leaders recognize when and how to take more of a back seat. Rather than always looking for ways to create more leaders, good leaders acknowledge and support the essential roles of those who follow.

Leaders should empower lower-level decision-making and translate strategy into a few clear and measurable outcomes that employees can understand, align with, and rally around. Decentralized decision-making generates timely and powerful market insights from employees on the front line who are navigating changing market conditions. "If you are a good leader, you will only make choices that you are definitely better equipped to make than anybody below you. It is your job to explain the rationale behind those choices to the next level and all the way down. Then leaders need to make it clear what choices everyone else has to make and the boundaries in which to make them," says strategy expert Roger Martin (Brightline Initiative, 2019).

### Organization-Wide Collaboration

Increasingly, the talk around organizations is of community, collaboration, ecosystems, and people working together. Leon Prieto and Simone Phipps have championed the idea of *cooperative advantage*—the notion that an organization's willingness to cooperate with others offers a distinctive competitive advantage in increasingly crowded global marketplaces. Resilience requires having the right individuals who can each do their own thing and, when needed, work well together. When the task requires it, teams can break down silos, add diversity to the creative process, and generate thinking and responsiveness far greater than the sum of individuals.

Care must be taken to craft such teams—whether from internal or external talent pools—with the right mix of capabilities and skill sets and explicitly set the conditions that enable people to work collectively. Successful leaders recognize that establishing effective collaboration takes time and deliberate coordination efforts. They also recognize the importance of incentivizing and forging processes that encourage and reward collaboration across organizational functions. Regardless of core structure, cross-functional teams are often viewed as the primary means in successful, organization-wide initiatives. Enhancing organization-wide collaboration that is focused on team performance rather than the individual can create a more flexible and responsive culture. It contributes to the ambidextrous strength of the organization, ultimately making it more resistant to changes in the business environment.

The bigger picture in collaboration is the changing nature of competition. Ron Adner, a professor at the Tuck School of Business at Dartmouth College and author of *The Wide Lens and Winning the Right Game*, argues that competitive rivalry is shifting from well-defined industries to broader ecosystems (Business Ecosystem Alliance, 2022). He explains: "COVID is a great example of an ecosystem disruption. It is something that in the old world, it's a virus, it's supposed to be solved within the realm of healthcare. Its impact broke through all these other boundaries. COVID is something that impacts international relations, trade, every function of government was impacted by COVID, and so the response to something like that can't just be within healthcare. The same is true of these other problems."

If collaboration crosses boundaries at strategic and competitive levels, then the willingness to embrace the perspectives and practices of others must begin within the organization. In other words, to be resilient, organizations must understand and practice collaboration at all levels. Consider how DBS Bank (DBS) has transformed itself partly through building ecosystems with partners. DBS realized that banking could no longer stand alone in a connected world (Speculand, 2021). As Robin Speculand describes, a key component of its 'Making Banking Joyful' strategy was starting to build ecosystems with partners. Before DBS's digital transformation, its business model was based on a network of branches, data centers, and customers reached through multiple products and services. Now, it focuses its business model on building ecosystems because banking can no longer stand alone in a connected world.

An extra challenge here is that collaboration is also an area that requires monitoring and management. Columbia Business School's Rita McGrath points out that companies, such as Samsung and Apple, compete with each other over patents and in the mobile phone market, yet work together elsewhere, with Samsung manufacturing many of Apple's products. "We're seeing much more the rise of what some people have called coopetition, where you compete in some markets and cooperate in others. You can't just be thinking about yourself and your own value chain, you've got to be thinking horizontally as well. Who else is in your arena? Who else is helping you add value to the customers?" says McGrath (Thinkers50, 2021).

## Mindset: Fearless and Humble

To build organizational resilience through culture, leaders need to instill the right mindset. Much of this relates to acceptance, trust, and recognition. "Companies frequently tell employees that collaboration is important, and then they force rank or assess them solely on the basis of their individual contributions," says Harvard Business School's Amy Edmondson, author of *The Fearless Organization*. "Employee evaluation needs to include rewards for cross-functional work so that people aren't faced with situations such as holding back ideas because they won't receive any credit for them."

To fully empower employees, leaders need to create a culture that embraces psychological safety and the acceptance of making mistakes. As pointed out by Edmondson, leaders need to value and model humility. This requires empathy and the ability to understand how difficult change can be for many people. Leaders also need to engage by coaching as well as embracing the different behaviors of employees.

One organization that successfully embraces and empowers employees is the global energy company Enel. Enel is now undergoing a deep transformation of its legacy model while driving the energy transition toward electrification and a sustainable future for all. Enel's Chief People & Organization Officer, Guido Stratta, has started a reinvention of the firm's management style and culture toward what he defines as *kind leadership*: moving from a bureaucratic command and control model to an empowering, motivating, and purposeful one based on mutual trust, creating the environment for people's passions and talents to bloom (Cervini & Rosani, 2022).

## Culture for Strategy

Strategy needs culture. Not only must culture support strategy, it must move in lockstep with a dynamic, evolving strategy where the behavioral recipe for winning is not fixed or static. While culture can neither be built directly nor accomplished through a blueprint or a checklist, it cannot be left to chance. It requires understanding the intricacy of culture as a dynamic and living organism made from the collective tension between individuals' behaviors and responses. Navigating that tension in an increasingly complex and changing environment depends on a shared sense of purpose and legitimate trust among employees. Coupling culture with strategy is a complicated and never-ending endeavor in shepherding influences, assessing outcomes, and adjusting the focus to building behavioral advantages that deliver winning strategies.

It is clear that our notion of what strategy is and how it impacts culture and resilience needs to change in many organizations. Roger Martin puts it this way:

Strategy is about imagining possibilities and then picking the one for which you have the strongest logic, not the strongest data. If we're teaching everybody in order to make business decisions, you must analyze the past then they will not invent the future. What's changed more than anything else is the domination of analysis in business decision making and that is the biggest threat to innovation and the suppressor of innovation in the modern business world. You've got to imagine possibility. Imagine a future that does not now exist. And if you are an excellent manager, you will figure out how to make that happen. We have a chance to do that. We've always had a chance to do that, but it's been suppressed over the last several decades. (Thinkers50, 2021)

And as an organization continues to sense trends and measure and monitor performance, there could be a need to strategize and make deliberate decisions to completely reimagine its business or to remain dormant while the destructive winds of a crisis blow and then for the organization to reemerge stronger and ready than ever to tackle future challenges.

Leadership, collaboration, mindset, and the ability to couple culture with strategy constitute a fertile ground for planting the seeds of resilient organizations. This has to be intentional and not left to chance. The time to begin is now.

## References

Brightline Initiative. (2018). *Brightline people manifesto*. https://www.brightline.org/people-manifesto/

Brightline Initiative. (2019). *Testing organizational boundaries to improve strategy execution*. https://www.brightline.org/resources/testing-organizational-boundaries-to-improve-strategy-execution/

Business Ecosystem Alliance (2022). *Winning the right game*. Webinar with Ron Adner, 23 March 2022. https://business-ecosystem-alliance.org/2022/03/25/winning-the-right-game/

Cervini, P., & Rosani, G. (2022). Radical reinvention. *Dialogue*. https://dialoguereview.com/radical-reinvention/

Crainer, S. (2000). *The management century*. Jossey-Bass.

Fischer, B. (2021). Relationships > assets: Haier's ecosystem revolution. *The Power of Ecosystems*. Thinkers50.

Speculand, R. (2021). *World's best bank: A strategic guide to digital transformation*. Bridges Business Consultancy.

Ruiz-Martin, C., López-Paredes, A., & Wainer, G. (2018). What we know and do not know about organizational resilience. *International Journal of Production Management and Engineering*, 6(1), 11–28.

Thinkers50. (2021). *The purpose of strategy*. Online event.

## About the Authors

**Emil Andersson, MSc,** is a strategy research consultant at Brightline®, a Project Management Institute (PMI) initiative. He is a practitioner in the fields of business strategy, transformation, and project management. Emil has been involved in over 40 global strategic projects and has a strong interest in disruptive technologies and how organizations create and deliver value.

**Tahirou Assane Oumarou, MASc, P.Eng., PMP,** is director of Brightline®, a Project Management Institute (PMI) initiative. He has over 20 years of experience in leadership roles, civil engineering, strategy, transformation, and project management. Previously, he worked as the deputy director of infrastructure and project management group in the United Nations Office for Project Services supporting the successful implementation of peace-building, humanitarian, and development projects around the world. He was also a senior project manager with the Ministry of Transportation in Ontario, Canada.

# How to Become Comfortable With Discomfort

SCOTT D. ANTHONY

2

To kick off discussions about navigating disruptive change, I asked group participants to pick which of nine images they associate with the current business environment. In the first half of 2022, about 1,000 people did the exercise. More than 50% of them picked images that had connotations of turbulence or struggle, namely a roller coaster (22%), a boat on stormy seas (17%), and an intense game of tug-of-war (14%). In contrast, only 17% of people picked the most optimistic images: a rocket ship taking off (9%), a calming image of rocks in water (4%), or a sailboat heading off into smooth water as the sun sets (3%). The discussion that typically follows surfaces collective angst about challenges, tensions, struggles, hardships, fatigue, and more.

While some might hold out hope that things will "get back to normal," in late 2021 *The Economist* demonstrated that memories of quiet, calm pre-pandemic life are false ones. "It is time to face the world's predictable unpredictability," the article noted (Economist, 2021). "The pattern for the rest of the 2020s is not the familiar routine of the pre-COVID years, but the turmoil and bewilderment of the pandemic era. The new normal is already here." We've been dealing with persistent uncertainty for decades and we'll be dealing with it forever more. The only constant, indeed, is change.

How do you build the organizational resilience to thrive in this era of predictable unpredictability? It comes down to another seemingly paradoxical phrase: being comfortable with discomfort. The text that follows describes practical pointers derived from the work my colleagues and I at Innosight have done over the past two decades, helping organizations around the world navigate disruptive change.

### Embrace Emergent Strategy

In 1985, Henry Mintzberg and James Waters published a paper that changed the field of strategy titled "Of Strategies Deliberate and Emergent." The paper contrasted two approaches to strategy (Mintzberg & Waters, 1985). **Deliberate** strategies involve planning and then acting. You thoroughly analyze strategic options by doing thorough research, talking to internal and external experts, and building sophisticated financial models. Once you identify the optimal strategy, you develop and carefully execute a deliberate plan to achieve your strategic ambitions.

A deliberate approach is rational and reasonable in stable conditions when you are competing against known competitors in a defined and measurable market. However, the approach is inappropriate in more fluid, uncertain circumstances. In these circumstances, the only certainty is that your first strategy will be wrong in some material way. The trick, then, is to learn *how* you are wrong as quickly and efficiently as possible.

Rather than planning and acting, emergent strategies are about testing and learning. Instead of gathering and analyzing data in search of the optimal option, an **emergent** strategy involves the design and execution of market-facing experiments. These experiments generate learning that, over time, allows the right strategy to emerge from the marketplace.

Emergent strategy is the essence of venture capital. While most entrepreneurs start with some kind of business plan, every venture capitalist knows that no business plan survives the first contact with reality. So, venture capitalists stage investment. Ventures that generate promising learning that suggest further potential get more funding; those that don't, don't.

An historical example helps to show emergent strategy in action. Back at the turn of the 20th century, the world was growing increasingly frustrated. Birds could fly. People could not. That had been the case for eternity, but over the past two centuries, scientific and industrial revolutions had ushered in the Machine Age. And, still, birds could fly. People could not.

The way most would-be aviators tried to address this challenge was to follow a deliberate approach. They analyzed the best available information to develop a clear viewpoint about the optimal approach to construct a flying machine. They worked diligently to build their machines, creating contraptions, which, in the hindsight of history, people would call crazy. They would then seek to fly. In some cases, failure required starting over. And for the brave souls who tested their ideas by jumping off cliffs or bridges....

Orville and Wilbur Wright—two bicycle merchants from the state of Ohio—followed an emergent approach. Before they tried to construct a plane, they built kites and gliders. The great thing about kites and gliders is when they crash—and in the early days of doing anything new, they always do—no one gets hurt and it is easy to try again. Digital tools have increasingly made it straightforward for people in a wide range of industries to enable low-risk experimentation with virtual *kites* such as quick protypes or focused test markets.

Kites can be purely analog as well. A few years ago, a toy company was thinking about launching a line of kiosks in hospitals. The company had seen the rise of kiosks selling electronic gizmos in airports and thought the high foot traffic in hospitals could create an attractive opportunity. The company could have spent hundreds of thousands of dollars building customized kiosks. Instead, it decided to do something much simpler. It set up a crude prototype of a toy kiosk. A TV monitor advertised products, a tablet device served as an order entry, the inventory was on a table, and fulfillment was done by Alasdair. Alasdair was not a lesser-known cousin of Siri and Alexa; he was an Innosight consultant who was advising the company. The kite crashed. It turned out that parents at hospitals weren't interested in buying toys. The company decided not to proceed with the idea. The good news was that it learned the idea wasn't viable quickly and cheaply.

The Wright Brothers were disciplined experimenters. In 1901, they combined a cardboard box, bicycle spoke wire, and a fan and created what we would now call a wind tunnel. As David McCollough described in his book *The Wright Brothers*:

> Though such apparatus did not look like much, it was to prove of immense value. For nearly two months the brothers tested some thirty-eight wing surfaces, setting the 'balances' or 'airfoils'—the different-shaped hacksaw blades—at angles from 0 to 45 degrees in winds up to 27 miles per hour. It was a slow, tedious process, but as Orville wrote, 'those metal models taught us how to build.' (McCollough, 2015).

Wilbur Wright later recalled that they learned that most of the mathematical assumptions other inventors were using about how different aspect ratios—the ratio between the wing's length and its span—would affect lift were full of errors. The lesson he took from the wind tunnel is that "sometimes the non-glamorous lab work is absolutely crucial to the success of a project."

If prototypes or test markets, like kites and gliders, are lower-risk ways to experiment, what is the modern equivalent of a wind tunnel, which makes experimentation easier and more efficient? Models and simulations are one tool increasingly used by companies. A laboratory stocked with tools helps too. Some companies have customers who agree to try out early versions of products and services. Or consider the simplest tool at your disposal: a thought experiment. Alfred Einstein famously credited the thought experiment of imagining himself running alongside a beam of light as inspiring his famous theory of relativity. Your thought experiment might not win you a Nobel Prize, but it can be a powerful way to learn about uncertain ideas. Place yourself in the shoes of your natural competitor and imagine how they might respond (also known as a *war game*). Repeat the exercise for a customer, channel partner, or salesforce member. Imagine how an innovator you admire might tackle the problem. Ask what would need to be true for an idea to be successful. These thought experiments don't cost anything but can provide critical learning.

Kites and wind tunnels allowed the Wright Brothers to learn a tremendous amount without taking undo risk or spending too much, helping them to create the craft that completed the first manned flight in 1903, ushering in the modern age of aviation.

## Back to Those Crashes

Another question I'll often ask groups is: What single word blocks innovation inside your organization? The word that appears most frequently is *fear*. As a father of four children, I can attest that our species is naturally curious and loves to experiment. Indeed, in the 1960s, George Land used an instrument designed for NASA to measure creativity and found that 98% of five-year-old children rated as creative geniuses (Land, 2011). However, when he tested adult populations, the percentage of creative geniuses dropped to 2%. Do people simply lose their innate curiosity and creativity?

I don't think so. Instead, they learn a progressive set of lessons that teach them that trying something different carries the risk of punishment. For example, a few years ago we received a threatening letter from the management of our condominium in Singapore describing an "incident" involving our children (a version of this incident appeared in the book I coauthored, *Eat, Sleep, Innovate*). They were captured on CCTV "vandalizing" the basketball court (Anthony et al., 2020). The letter described how, fortunately, the cleaners removed the stains, "otherwise we would have to claim all damages from you." What materials did our children use on the Sunday afternoon in question? Yes, it was chalk. The kids were bored and asked if they could go down to the basketball court and draw a diamond and play baseball. Not only did dad approve, if the CCTV image were higher quality, I would have been implicated in the letter as well. And it wasn't valiant cleaners who removed the "stains." It was the skies, as a typical afternoon thunderstorm washed away all evidence of the chalk incident.

Zoom into a potential creative genius sitting on the court that day: my then five-year-old son Harry. What lesson does the chalk incident teach the happy-go-lucky, insatiably curious boy, known at school by the nickname "Happy

Harry?" That creative expression—even innocent creative expression—carries the risk of being slapped on the wrist. When he goes to school, he will learn there are right and wrong answers to tests. When he goes to work, he will learn that there are right and wrong ways to do things. Like all humans, he suffers from an innate bias called *loss aversion*, where he would rather avoid losses than receive equivalent gains. The natural curiosity and desire to experiment will slowly but surely be conditioned out of him.

Bringing out the *Happy Harrys* in your organization requires celebrating, rather than castigating, intelligent failure. Note the use of *intelligent* as an adjective in the previous sentence. I was conducting a workshop for a leading European bank a couple of years ago and I asked attendees if they could provide any examples of intelligent failure. "For sure!" one person responded. "About a decade ago, we threw about €1 billion down the drain on an idea that almost blew up the financial system. That was a doozie!" Amy Edmondson from the Harvard Business School would call this a *preventable* failure (Edmondson, 2019). That happens when people don't do their homework, smartly stage experimentation, or contain the risks of their efforts. Preventable failure should be swiftly and severely punished. *Intelligent failure*, on the other hand, is when someone identifies an exciting but uncertain opportunity, designs smart experiments to learn about key uncertainties, bounds the risks of those experiments, and learns that one of their key assumptions was wrong. Yes, we have to call that a failure, but history shows repeatedly that learning from intelligent failure often paves the way for future successes.

Consider Innosight X. A few years ago, our Innosight team in Asia spent close to two years working on a digital platform, which we hoped would open up new market opportunities. We experimented with a range of different business models. One idea involved having short sprints where users would watch videos, use tools, and be guided by experts to tackle common innovation challenges. Another model was one using the digital platform to facilitate group projects with noncompetitive, smaller companies. A third model was to license digital intellectual property (IP) to consultants looking for competitive differentiation. None of these ideas gained traction, so we eventually shut the effort down.

A failure, right? Not exactly. Although the consortium model didn't take off, it surfaced the opportunity to develop a new pricing and delivery model that leveraged Innosight's IP to provide more focused support to clients. This offering grew to constitute a significant portion of Innosight's revenue in 2021.

Innovation is something different that creates value. Because it is different you can't be sure you will succeed. Even the smartest people get it wrong sometimes. For example, in 2020 I had a chance to interview one of my heroes: Ed Catmull. The cofounder and long-term CEO of Pixar Animation Studios is a legend in the field of innovation. He has won everything from an Oscar to the Turing Award for contributions of lasting and major technical importance to computer science. He literally wrote the book on how you build a culture that encourages creativity, *Creativity Inc.*, a must-read book coauthored by Amy Wallace. I interviewed Catmull in late 2020 tied to the launch of *Eat, Sleep, Innovate*. It turns out even the great Ed Catmull is wrong a significant amount of the time.

"I realized that about two-thirds of the things that I tried to do were right and one-third of them just were wrong," Catmull said. "It is very good for leaders just to say to themselves, 'I'm experienced, I'm here for a reason, but a third of what I'm thinking, or what I believe, is a complete crock.'"

One of the greatest innovators of our time self admits to being wrong one third of the time. And feels good about it! Release the Happy Harrys in your organization, or in yourself, by recognizing that failure is often a stepping-stone to success so you should encourage—no, *celebrate*—intelligent failure.

## Killing Zombies

Another factor that people report holds back their innovation efforts is a lack of resources. Our experience has been that almost every organization has more resources to invest in innovation than it realizes. If, that is, the organization is willing to confront a malicious plague. The plague of the zombie project. The walking undead. The projects that if you are really honest with yourself will never materially move the growth needle, but still shuffle and linger on, sucking all of the innovation life out of an organization.

The essence of strategy, whether it be in times of comforting stability or radical uncertainty, is choice. What you choose to do, and what you choose not to do.

In a 2010 Fast Company conference, newly minted Nike CEO Mark Parker described a fascinating discussion he had with Steve Jobs from Apple. Parker, who went on to have a brilliant run over the next eight years as he drove digitalization within the iconic apparel company, received a congratulatory call from Jobs soon after being named CEO. Parker saw it as an opportunity to get advice from the iconic leader. "Nike makes some of the best products in the world. Products that you lust after, absolutely beautiful, stunning products," Parker reported Jobs said. "But you also make a lot of crap. Just get rid of the crappy stuff and focus on the good stuff."(Gallo, 2010) Parker then noted that he expected a pause and a laugh. There was a pause, but there was no laugh, because Jobs was dead serious.

We often forget this chapter of the Steve Jobs story. People remember Jobs the Creator, birthing the iPod, iPhone, iPad, and Apple Store. But when Jobs returned as CEO of Apple in the late 1990s, he started as *Jobs the Destroyer*. He streamlined the product portfolio down to four products, so Apple had space to innovate and grow.

Rita McGrath from the Columbia Business School provides timeless advice for how to put zombies down, noting the importance of precisely defined criteria, independent participants, and rigorous knowledge capture and transfer (McGrath, 2011). Killing zombies in a humane way—getting rid of the crappy stuff so you can focus on the good stuff—is a key enabler of innovation-driven growth (Anthony et al., 2015).

## Transcending the Socratic Paradox

Philosophers have long pondered the famous Socratic paradox, derived from Plato's account of the ancient Greek philosopher. "I know," the paradox goes, "that I know nothing." How does that paradox make you feel? Perhaps you feel paralyzed. If you know nothing, what can you possibly do in a world of uncertainty? Why not choose to feel empowered? Embrace a fundamental humility and learning orientation—what modern researchers would call a growth mindset. That mindset helps to transcend the Socratic paradox, setting you on a life-long journey of discovery and innovation.

Remember the parable of the two shoe salespeople who arrive in a remote village where no one is wearing shoes. The one with the fixed mindset who sees nothing but limitations sags their shoulders. "There's no market here. I came all this way for nothing. I'm going home." The one with the growth mindset sees possibility and potential. "The market is totally wide open! I better call headquarters and ask for more shoes!"

Remember, today's ambiguity creates tomorrow's opportunity (Anthony, 2016). Fly kites. Build wind tunnels. Celebrate intelligent failure. Kill zombies. And never, ever stop innovating!

## References

Anthony, S. D., Duncan, D. S., & Siren, P. M. A. (2015). Zombie projects: How to find them and kill them. *Harvard Business Review*. March. https://hbr.org/2015/03/zombie-projects-how-to-find-them-and-kill-them

Anthony, S. D. (2016). How to turn ambiguity into opportunity: A new approach to strategy under uncertainty. Innosight, Summer 2016. https://www.innosight.com/wp-content/uploads/2017/11/How-to-Turn-Ambiguity-into-Opportunity-A-New-Approach-to-Strategy-under-Uncertainty1.pdf

Anthony, S. D., Cobban, P., Painchaud, N., & Parker, A. (2020). *Eat, sleep, innovate: How to make creativity an everyday habit inside your organization.* Harvard Business Review Press.

*Economist*. (December 18, 2021). The new normal is already here. Get used to it. *The Economist*. https://www.economist.com/leaders/2021/12/18/the-new-normal-is-already-here-get-used-to-it

Edmondson, A. C. (2019). *The fearless organization: Creating psychological safety in the workplace for learning, innovation, and growth.* John Wiley & Sons.

Gallo, C. (2010). Steve Jobs's strategy? 'Get rid of the crappy stuff'. *Fast Company*. October 8.

Land, G. (2011). *The failure of success.* TedXTuscon, Youtube.com. https://www.youtube.com/watch?v=ZfKMq-rYtnc&t=1s

McCollough, D. (2015). *The Wright brothers*. Simon & Schuster.

McGrath, R. G. (2011). Failing by design. *Harvard Business Review*.

Mintzberg, H., & Waters, J. (1985). Of strategies, deliberate and emergent. *Strategic Management Journal*, 6(1985), 257.

## About the Author

**Scott D. Anthony** is Clinical Professor at the Tuck School of Business at Dartmouth and a Senior Partner at Innosight, a growth strategy consultancy. Ranked by Thinkers50 as one of the world's leading management thinkers, he is coauthor of *Eat, Sleep, Innovate: How to Make Creativity an Everyday Habit Inside Your Organization* (Harvard Business Review Press, 2020). His previous books are *Dual Transformation; The First Mile: A Launch Manual for Getting Great Ideas Into the Market; Seeing What's Next: Using the Theories of Innovation to Predict Industry Change* (with Innosight cofounder and Harvard Professor Clayton Christensen); *The Innovator's Guide to Growth: Putting Disruptive Innovation to Work; The Silver Lining: An Innovation Playbook for Uncertain Times; The Little Black Book of Innovation: How It Works, How to Do It;* and *Building a Growth Factory.*

# Risk Management is the Key to Innovation

JONATHAN BRILL

3

The COVID-19 pandemic has frightened a lot of business leaders. Not only has it disrupted their immediate plans but it has created new uncertainties (will people return to offices, will inflation persist?) and dangers (what if we have to pay substantially more for talent, what if another pandemic hits?) Risk is on everyone's mind these days, but we think about it in the wrong way.

Investment risk is measured by beta, the expected amount of change over time. It's not just a measure of threat. As we learned in Business 101, it's also an indicator of opportunity—for the prepared. More billionaires are minted during financial disruptions than in good times. If you can figure out a way to take on beta more cheaply than your customers, either through scale or technology, you've got the makings of a strong business model. Not just in insurance, but in a wide range of industries. Facebook, for example, is highly profitable because its analytics reduce much of the uncertainty in advertising by flexibly targeting ads to relevant viewers.

What we have long suspected, but recently confirmed, is that companies that play the long game are more profitable over time. A major reason for this is that they tend to invest in resilience even at the cost of some quarterly performance. Those that don't are suffering. Enterprise risk management has matured as a field, but it hasn't delivered: eight of the 10 largest publicly held American corporations failed to identify a pandemic as a material risk.

In too many of these companies, the people involved in risk management and innovation are like organizational oil and water, never collaborating. But when mixed together, risk management techniques empower both process and product innovation: by identifying internal and external pain points and providing tools to take bigger risks. To maximize the benefits of game-changing innovation, companies need to integrate their work on resilience and growth.

Here's a framework for using risk management tools to do exactly that. Start with the four areas of your business that are most likely to be impacted by change—what I call the four FOES (financial, operational, external, and strategic)—see Figure 1—and add the four underlying dynamics—risk switches in Figure 2—that can change your risk profile.

| F | O | E | S |
|---|---|---|---|
| **Financial** | **Operational** | **External** | **Strategic** |
| Financial Strategy | Earnings | Input Costs | Demand Forecasts |
| Asset Losses | Input costs | Political Shifts | Leadership Changes |
| Goodwill | IT Security | Government Regulation | Governance Priorities |
| Amortization | Accounting | Litigation | Pricing Issues |
| Liquidity | Capacity | Local Economics | Competition |
| Debt & Interest | Supply Chain | International Economics | Product Performance |
| | Fraud and Theft | Natural Disasters | Regulation |
| | Noncompliance | Pandemics | R&D |
| | Budgeting | Armed Conflict | Customer Satisfaction |
| | Financial Controls | Partner Losses | M&A Integration |
| | Supplier Availability | Credit Rating | Investor Guidance |
| | Workplace Safety | Industry Crisis | |
| | Systems Failures | | |

**Figure 1.** The four FOES.

When aspects of the environment change, they affect the FOES. Risk managers track the FOES to identify threats. Innovation managers often fail to grasp that these also point to opportunities for innovation.

| **Static** | | **Dynamic** |
|---|---|---|
| Probability is constant | ··········· versus ··········· | Probability changes |
| **Symmetric** | | **Asymmetric** |
| Impacts all parts equally | ··········· versus ··········· | Impacts parties differently |
| **Synchronous** | | **Asynchronous** |
| Impacts all parties simultaneously | ··········· versus ··········· | Impacts parties at different times |
| **Sustained** | | **Temporary** |
| Ongoing impact | ··········· versus ··········· | Transient impact |

**Figure 2.** Risk switches.

## The four risk switches can flip back and forth:

**From dynamic to static:** Insurers use their scale and diversification to take on ever-changing (dynamic) risks so they can keep premiums constant (static) even if, for example, a forest fire erupts near a customer's house.

**From symmetric to asymmetric:** In supply chains, Toyota adjusted its innovative Lean methodology to allow stockpiling of crucial parts, such as semiconductors, giving it an advantage over rivals when symmetric risks (the Taiwan earthquake and then the COVID-19 pandemic) disrupted supplies.

**From synchronous to asynchronous:** Visa gave households enormous flexibility by scaling up credit cards that people could pay off when they chose (asynchronous), not just when making purchases (synchronous).

**From sustained to temporary:** With their research into mRNA-based vaccines, BioNTech and Moderna turned COVID-19, which could have become a much worse sustained economic crisis (until reaching herd immunity), into something that has rapidly become manageable.

Innovators can use what I call Innovation Bingo, outlined in Figure 3, to rapidly map out new opportunities. First look at the combinations of Financial, Operational, External, and Strategic changes that create the most uncertainty for you and your customers—then consider which risk switches you can flip to increase the chance of a positive outcome.

Let's see how innovators have used Innovation Bingo to turn threats into opportunities.

|  | Financial | Operational | External | Strategic |
|---|---|---|---|---|
| Dynamic versus Static |  |  |  |  |
| Symmetric versus Asymmetric |  |  |  |  |
| Synchronous versus Asynchronous |  |  |  |  |
| Sustained versus Temporary |  |  |  |  |

**Figure 3.** Innovation bingo.

## From Buggy Whips to Perfume

Consider France's Hermès, a brand that should have died a century ago. Look at their logo: a gentleman with a horse and carriage. The family-run business was France's leader in buggy whips when automobiles rolled out in the 1910s. But it didn't stand still, even as the number of horses in Europe decreased by 90% by midcentury. They responded to this dynamic threat by acquiring the European license for zippers (the "*fermeture Hermès*" in France). They applied their leather expertise and high-culture brand to new products such as sports jackets. Their famous silk scarves were another experiment. They reduced the risk of economic volatility in postwar France by setting up shops in the United States. They also licensed watches from the Swiss brand Universal Genève. What had been symmetric risks for leather goods in Europe became asymmetric. Hermès was insulated from the worst of these trends, but its regional competitors suffered.

As consumer spending took off in the 1960s, Hermès diversified into perfume and became one of the first, true lifestyle brands. When synthetic materials began to dominate and commoditize its mainstay products, the firm doubled down on the luxury segment, selling python skin jackets and ostrich skin jeans at outrageous prices. It then went into glassware, silverware, and a variety of home furnishings. The company continues to live in the fickle world of fashion, yet has little fear of its goods in such diverse categories going out of style at the same time. Hermès was worth billions in its 1993 Initial Public Offering—while still making its classic leather riding crops for equestrians.

Perhaps unconsciously, the Hermès-Dumas family who owned Hermès thus addressed several areas of the Innovation Bingo map. Mass automobile markets threatened not just the firm but also its prime customers, people wealthy enough to need horse harnesses and whips. How would they uphold their class distinctions when most people could afford personal transportation? By applying their expertise in craftsmanship and style to a range of innovative products, Hermès provided the markers that helped those customers maintain their sense of distinctness and fine living.

Hermès thus turned a sustained risk into a temporary one—customers needed to reorient their consumption around new class markers. For social climbers, especially in the booming 1960s, Hermès likewise turned a dynamic risk 'How can I stay aware of what the upper classes are wearing?' into a static one 'I can regularly patronize the offerings of Hermès at its many global stores'.

## From Farm Commodities to Four-Leaf Clovers

Similarly, The Chef's Garden started out as an ordinary family farm in Milan, Ohio, an hour's drive west of Cleveland. Like their neighbors, the Jones family planted the commodity crops common to the area such as soybeans and corn. But in the 1980s, the combination of high inflation and a bad storm bankrupted their business. In the intervening years, an increasingly hostile environment has caused many small farms to give up. In Ohio as a whole, big corporations now own 86% of the farmland.

Rather than sell out, the Joneses switched their business model. As creditors auctioned off much of their farmland and equipment, the family planted niche crops for restaurants, where quality and variety matter more than low prices. They had to learn new farming methods, invest in new tools, and invent new types of greenhouses. But it worked, and today The Chef's Garden is a major purveyor of specialty produce not just to Cleveland, but around the world.

The Joneses flipped most of the risk switches. Instead of growing all of their crops in a single season and then selling them, no matter where the markets stood (synchronous), they delivered different crops every week of the year (asynchronous). They went from a static product line of a few crops to a dynamic one of about 600—with the bottom 200 products discontinued each year to make way for an equal number of experiments. They helped popularize microgreens and now they're experimenting with white strawberries that have red seeds.

Instead of going head-to-head in symmetric competition against the Big Agriculture companies that scooped up Ohio farmland, they developed an asymmetric strategy. Rather than sell massive amounts of wheat just to break even, they make money selling a few buckets of four-leaf clovers to bars in Las Vegas, Nevada.

That flexible business model helped them survive even as the COVID-19 pandemic shut down their main customers, restaurants. They pivoted quickly to consumers, where home chefs were trying all sorts of unusual recipes and looking for hard-to-get items. Direct selling to households has been a challenge, but they've actually sold more vegetables by weight than they did to restaurants before COVID-19. And now they've done the hard work of understanding that audience, so they can maintain it profitably as their historic business, restaurant customers, comes back.

Both Hermès and the Jones family farm were hit with challenges that could have been caused by a broad range of disruptions. Instead of focusing on individual risks, they chose to innovate in ways that benefited them no matter what the change. Innovation almost always starts in an ambiguous place and much of it fails due to poorly defined goals. In our increasingly volatile world, a framework like Innovation Bingo can help prioritize your efforts and get a leg up on your competition. Resilience is more than the key to survival; it's also the key to growth.

## About the Author

**Jonathan Brill** is a globally recognized expert, advisor, and speaker on successful innovation under uncertainty. He was the Global Futurist at HP, Creative Director at Frog, and the managing partner of innovation firms that generated US$27 billion in new revenue for clients. Brill is the author of *Rogue Waves: Future–Proof Your Business to Survive and Profit From Radical Change* (McGraw-Hill, 2021). He speaks at and provides thought leadership through Harvard and Stanford Universities, TED, SXSW, J.P. Morgan, the Global Peter Drucker Forum, *Harvard Business Review*, *The Financial Times*, *South China Morning Post, Forbes*, Korn Ferry, the *Economist Global Report* and Thinkers50.

Learn more and find tools at jonathanbrill.com. Contact him at jonathan@jonathanbrill.com.

# Building Resilience by Leading Change

CHRIS CLEARFIELD

4

It's easy to imagine a world where, if only we knew enough, life would be predictable. We could get a handle on our work, succeed in all endeavors, and finally have time to do all the things we want to do.

But that world is an illusion.

As the systems that run the world grow more sophisticated, they tend to increase in complexity. That complexity allows us to accomplish difficult, seemingly unachievable tasks—often without needing to know much more than how to click a button. But as our systems get more capable, they also become more interlinked and harder to change.

Even leaders at the top of their organizations can't simply decree improvement. Rather, they need to shift people, processes, and technology to move their organizations in new directions. That's a critical skill, because the world of modern business isn't static. We don't win by digging a deeper moat or building bigger walls to cement our positions. Rather, we win by building organizations that thrive because of their ability to learn and adapt.

Resiliency is the ability to change course in response to pressure and potential catastrophe. It's not a single strategy but a shift in attitude and capabilities. It requires a willingness to change, even in the face of great success. And one thing we all know from being human is that change is hard—whether we're changing what we offer to our clients, how our teams work, or even how we show up as a leader.

The reality is that we always get value from the way we work now. Our organizations are perfectly set up to create exactly the output we're getting—even if we don't like that output anymore. If you do what you've always done, you will get what you've always gotten, right?

I work with a lot of sophisticated leaders—lawyers, doctors, programmers, engineers, and safety professionals—who have moved, in their leadership journey, from solving purely *technical* problems to solving *sociotechnical* problems.

Technical problems aren't easy to solve, but they are solvable. We find a workable way of moving forward, implement our solution, and move on. We find the right *thing*—a contract, treatment, technology, material, or procedure—implement it, and move on.

Sociotechnical problems, on the other hand, are never really solved. They have a technical component and a human component. People are involved and when we're solving problems with people, their preferences, opinions, fears, and uncertainties matter. People are parts of organizations, teams, and departments that work in a certain way and derive a benefit from their current approach (even if there's an associated cost).

Consider my client Jon. An engineer by training, Jon is a senior executive at a major manufacturing company. He has decades of operational experience, with accountability over several major manufacturing facilities, including one of the largest plants of its kind in the United States.

Jon's company faced a problem. Over time, it had grown overly bureaucratic and less competitive. As a result, costs increased and, despite complex procedures designed to ensure a reliable manufacturing process, quality had not improved.

The market had also changed. Jon's company relied on a business model that required scale to be profitable, while many of its end users were looking for more product customization, which required smaller manufacturing runs.

Unless Jon's company could shift its approach, it risked slipping into irrelevance. Jon's senior leadership recognized the threat they faced, but they weren't sure what to do about it.

Jon was offered a role catalyzing innovation across global manufacturing. Excited, he recruited a team to research and analyze the company's challenges. For almost a year, he and his team of eight engineers dug into their data and identified a few key changes that manufacturing plants could make to simultaneously increase agility, improve quality, and save money. This would help his firm make the changes they needed to compete despite the forces disrupting their industry.

Despite his evidence-driven approach, Jon's efforts to drive the adoption of these new practices were met with resistance. And using more data and stronger arguments didn't work. Over time, Jon and his team became frustrated and demoralized.

Daunted, Jon reached out to me. "I don't understand why people don't see what needs to be done," he lamented. "How can I make other people see the answer?"

That's a seductive question. If we could just get other people to recognize that we're right, things would be a lot easier.

Unfortunately, when we're working on sociotechnical problems, it's not the right question. To advance a complex problem, we need to lead by creating *possibilities* instead of imposing answers. Indeed, as we began our work together, Jon began to see that trying to force his answer onto others was part of the problem.

The leaders I work with do counterintuitive things to catalyze lasting change. First, they stop pushing people toward an answer. Instead, they practice curiosity and encourage those around them to do the same. Second, they let go of the view that there is one right answer. Instead, these leaders view change as a journey to undertake with others. Finally, they learn to manage the discomfort that arises for them and their organizations when they declare they don't know the answer.

## Get Curious

When I ask leaders to raise their hands if they like being told what to do, almost every arm stays down.

The desire for autonomy and independence goes deep. Anyone with kids (not that kids are a *great* model for senior leadership) will recognize that resisting control is an important part of being a person, yet control is the tool that leaders often reach for: We mandate changes, roll out new approaches without consulting people who will be affected, and then act surprised when we face resistance.

That's exactly what happened to Jon. Despite his technical credibility and decades of operational experience, plant managers viewed him as a distraction or, worse, a corporate lackey who had lost touch with what it was like to run a plant.

Resistance isn't, in itself, bad. But resistance becomes a problem when we try to push through it without understanding it. That's because resistance grows in strength when we ignore it. When we spend time and effort persuading people and making our case by marshaling mounds of data that support our decisions, we're left with more resistance.

Anytime you're trying to overcome resistance, anytime you're looking for buy-in—you've already lost!

Instead of trying to overcome resistance, we can learn to see it as something to understand and celebrate. Resistance is a clue that we're missing something, a sign that we need to ask more questions, questions such as:

- What is the story we're telling ourselves?
- How confident are we that our story is true?
- What can we learn from people who don't like our ideas?
- How can their perspective help us arrive at a better outcome?

Working with resistance means leading from a place of curiosity: asking questions without being invested in the answers you get. Instead, it's listening with openness, without advocating for a particular path or solution, and creating space for others to share their insights. In doing so, you can see the challenge *as it actually is*.

Asking curious questions is like doing aerobics—you don't get better by watching other people do it. It's a muscle that needs exercise. You've got to practice. And, like all exercise routines, starting out can feel uncomfortable.

If you work in an organization that's really good at giving answers and delivering PowerPoint decks full of data, as Jon did, it may be challenging to go out and engage with people instead of *pushing* answers onto them.

When we admit that we don't know the answer and become interested in what others think, we can step back from the need to be right and open ourselves to being influenced by others. By embracing curiosity, we won't get stuck in dogma. We can cocreate a path that didn't exist before. Paradoxically, by not pushing as hard, by being more open, we can move faster. In curiosity, we find a better way to lead change.

As Jon learned, leaders can't make people listen. While we might compel behaviors or shift incentives, that gets us compliance, at best. But we can engage others and invite them to join us in our vision.

## Change is a Journey

Many of the leaders I work with are impatient. They've advanced in their careers by coming up with the right answer and getting things done quickly. Like Jon, by the time they're tasked with leading a big change, many of them have spent years thinking about the problem and they're ready for results.

But instead of driving people to your version of the answer, you can drastically improve your effectiveness at leading change by inviting them on your journey.

To do this, you'll start by spending time exploring the problem with those you are asking to change. You might have a well-developed idea of the problem you face; you may even have studied it and have data to back up your conclusions. By all means, share some of the ways you see the challenge, but before you proceed, pause, and ask others how they see it. Learn how the challenge affects them and what aspects of it they care about. Be open to the possibility that your mental model of the problem—often developed in the comfort of a corporate office—may not match the experiences of those actually doing the work.

A rule of thumb I use for my clients is that, toward the beginning of their engagement process, they should be sharing what they see 25% of the time and listening 75% of the time. As your change gains momentum and you start to cocreate solutions in your organization, the proportions will shift closer to 50-50.

This is easy to imagine in a one-on-one conversation, but you can structure groups to encourage participation. For example, when I'm designing conversations, I will often ask a question, have everyone think about it for a minute or two, group people into pairs for a discussion, combine the pairs into foursomes to compare notes, and then debrief the themes in the whole group.

Only when you've reached a mutual understanding about the challenge you face can you start to think about solutions. Showing up with a perspective balanced with curiosity sets a tone of cooperation. By not claiming to have "The Answer," you draw others to you and create space for their creativity. Once possibilities start to emerge, your job is to create more space to test them.

When you seek to understand people and work together to cocreate solutions, you bring them along on your journey. You go from an imposing figure to an inviting one, from an adversary to a guide.

But, to make that transition, you also have to make an internal shift: you have to be okay admitting you don't know the answer.

## Get Comfortable Being Uncomfortable

When I mentor younger professionals, they often have the idea that once people reach the executive ranks, they will be able to relax because they will suddenly know all the answers.

Nothing could be further from the truth. In many ways, the pressure to have an answer gets worse as you rise in the ranks of a company. Having an answer makes us feel secure and it removes the discomfort of not knowing. When leading a complex change, however, the value of answers is limited.

Answers exist in an email, report, or PowerPoint deck, but they don't create change; they are nothing if they're not brought to life. It's easy, as Jon did, to come up with an answer and then be frustrated that others aren't listening to you.

Yet we often hold fast to our answer-based paradigm. Even when answers don't solve our problems, they make us feel better. The search for answers creates a sense of busyness that distracts us from our fear of uncertainty. Pushing for movement in any direction feels good—even if it turns out we're just treading water.

Instead of reaching for answers, we have to develop something called *negative capability*. Negative capability is a term coined by the poet John Keats in an 1817 letter—it's our ability to stay in a state of uncertainty without an "irritable reaching after facts." It's about being okay with not having an immediate answer and accepting the unknown.

When leading change, your job isn't to know the answer, it's to create the conditions for a solution to emerge. For many leaders, that shift is hard because it requires embracing your vulnerability.

But, with a little support, many of the leaders I work with find great relief in letting go of the idea that everything rests on their shoulders. When Jon let go of the need to impose an answer on others, he told me he felt lighter.

For others, the realization that they don't need to control all the details means they can keep their heads above water and think in visionary terms rather than getting mired in the details. These leaders are still accountable for the success of their changes, but that doesn't mean they have to be those inventing and imposing solutions on their team members through sheer force of will.

## Conclusion

Leaders of resilient organizations adapt to changing conditions even as they enjoy success. They recognize there are no simple answers to complex problems.

When facing a complex problem, the solution is rarely more data or more technology but rather the willingness to embrace complexity and work with others in open and collaborative ways.

These three shifts—leaning into curiosity, bringing others along on your journey, and getting comfortable with not knowing—are different from the typical approach of decreeing a new way of working, rolling it out across an organization, and being disappointed by the results.

This human-centered approach to change works best when you start with a small but willing group. Jon started by engaging a plant manager he knew well. Once they achieved success in that plant, word spread. Others got curious about their work and started asking for help. Along the way, Jon and his team grew more adept at leading change and building momentum across the entire organization.

The leaders I coach practice new ways of working that fundamentally change their organizations. These shifts seem simple on paper, but that doesn't make them easy. Curiosity requires practice. Guiding people on a journey requires patience, and admitting you don't know the answer requires the courage to be vulnerable.

The good news is that leaders like you *can* make these changes. You just have to start by getting curious—and, sometimes, getting a little support along the way.

To learn more about how my team and I support leaders catalyzing transformational change in their organizations, go to http://clearfieldgroup. com/resilience.

## About the Author

**Chris Clearfield** is the cofounder and chief executive of the Clearfield Group, where he helps leaders guide transformational change. He works with engineers, software developers, safety professionals, attorneys, and C-suite executives. As a coach and consultant, he supports leaders in attending to the social *and* technical aspects of their work to solve their unique and complex challenges in creative, collaborative ways.

Clearfield is the coauthor of *Meltdown: What Plane Crashes, Oil Spills, and Dumb Business Decisions Can Teach Us About How to Succeed at Work and at Home* (Penguin Press, 2018), which was named a best book of 2018 by *The Financial Times* and won the National Business Book Award.

Clearfield works on risk, strategy, and innovation with leaders at some of the world's most interesting companies, from major oil producers and professional service firms to tech companies such as Etsy, Netflix, and Microsoft. He's a graduate of Harvard University, where he studied physics and biochemistry.

# The Agile Organization's Secret: Operating Models

EDIVANDRO CARLOS CONFORTO

5

**O**ur perception about the speed of change has certainly evolved over the years. In fact, change has been part of our lives since the beginning of the universe. On the business side it is true that we are facing a more chaotic environment, where stability is a luxury item that many organizations cannot afford.

You need to adapt, and fast! All sorts of businesses need to become more resilient! After the COVID-19 pandemic crisis, we entered the decade of business agility, since many paradoxical, structural, and behavioral changes were triggered by the pandemic and were implemented at lightning speed in many organizations.

Several studies have reported the benefits of adopting agility at all levels, including better financial performance, long-term and sustainable growth, innovation, resiliency, flexibility, customer satisfaction, people culture, and behavior.

Today, every organization wants to *be agile*, not just *do agile* in order to become more resilient. However, besides technology adoption, there is something even more critical and is the secret of the most successful agile companies I know: their operating model. According to Accenture research, operating models have been on the agendas of C-suite executives for a while (Accenture Research, 2022). The research found that 93% of C-suite executives surveyed thought their existence was jeopardized by operating models that cannot keep pace, and at least seven out of 10 respondents felt they would need to completely rethink their operating models to be more resilient as a result of the COVID-19 pandemic.

By implementing the right operating model, organizations can achieve a perpetual state of transformation and will enable business agility capabilities critical to the growth and sustainability of the business (Conforto & Mendes, 2022). A successful operating model will help organizations deliver what I call the 3A's of agility: *anticipate, adapt,* and *accelerate.*

**Anticipate** means we are envisioning and experimenting the future, while balancing opposing forces such as predictability and innovation. **Adapt** means that the organization has the flexibility and speed to learn, make the right decisions, and improve continuously. Finally, **accelerate** means that the organization is capable of reducing time to market and lead time, with a relentless focus on delivering value to customers.

In essence, agility is a capability—neither a method nor a technology—and has different dimensions (product, service, operations, and business) and is dependent on multiple factors, including culture, processes, and technology (see Figure 1).

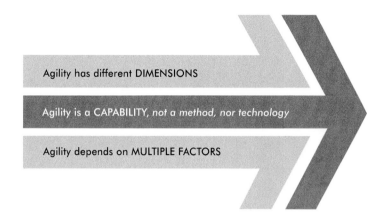

**Figure 1.** The essence of agility.

Source: Adapted from Conforto, E.C., et al (2016). The agility construct on project management theory. *International Journal of Project Management* 34.4, pp. 660-674.

These concepts are essential if your organization wants to develop the right operating model. It is not my intention to be exhaustive in the discussion on how to create and implement a successful operating model; this will require the whole book to explain. Rather, I want to share practical insights on what to look for when building your own operating model.

Operating models are highly dependent on many factors related to the business, its customer needs, and market characteristics. In this article, I want to contribute my experience and some elements present in most operating models. I have found these to be successful in their mission to deliver strategic results consistently, and keep the pace of transformation in more resilient organizations.

## Building Your Operating Model

Gartner defines an operating model as the blueprint for how value will be created and delivered to target customers (Gartner, 2022). An operating model brings the business model to life; it supports the execution of the business model, which is different from an information and technology (I&T) operating model, defined as how an organization orchestrates its information and technology capabilities to achieve its strategic objectives. In this article, I want to address the more comprehensive understanding of an operating model that also encompasses IT capabilities.

Before we jump into the discussion, it is important to highlight that every company should build its own operating model, that trying to copy others will not guarantee any success and, most importantly, there is no one-size-fits-all approach to designing and implementing an operating model.

Having said that, let us take a look at these four characteristics, which I've seen present in most successful operating models: (1) organized by value stream, (2) the right team structure, (3) agile governance, and (4) a culture of autonomy.

## Organized by Value Stream

The most successful and modern operating models originate in value streams. A business may have different value streams; for example, in a manufacturing company, you might find some examples such as insight into strategy, order to cash, concept to development, and so forth. For each value stream, there are several integrated, interdependent elements, including information, people, technology, and tools and practices.

In the classic book, *Lean Thinking: Banish Waste and Create Wealth in Your Corporation* (1996) by James P. Womack and Daniel T. Jones who contributed to disseminating the concept of value streams, the authors shared a key premise to organize work around value streams:

> Just as activities that cannot be measured can't be properly managed, the activities necessary to create, order, and produce a specific product (or service), which can't be precisely identified, analyzed, and linked together cannot be challenged, improved (or eliminated altogether), and, eventually, perfected. p. 37

Womack and Jones observe that the great majority of management attention has historically gone to managing aggregates—such as processes, departments, firms—and overseeing many products at once. Yet, what is missing most of the time, and is really needed, is managing whole value streams for specific goods and services. In addition, leaders should view value streams as one of the main foundational elements that help the organization achieve a more efficient and lean status through an operational and strategic approach to delivering value (Hines et al., 1998).

Here are some steps to defining an operating model oriented by value streams:
- Clearly identify the business purpose and business drivers.
- Identify business value streams first—products or service families.
- Identify pain points of the value stream.

- Identify macroprocesses and key performance indicators (KPIs).
- Identify the systems that support the products or service families.
- Identify the teams and people.
- Map and detail the whole value stream.

You can implement these steps in your organization, taking as a starting point some generic value streams present in most companies. Examples may include, but are not limited to:
- Product design to market
- Contracting to registration
- Invoicing to payment
- Order to cash

Be mindful that making this change (turning into a value stream-oriented operating model) will trigger many other changes in the organization, such as definitions of roles and responsibilities, performance assessment, and governance; and even some reorganization will be necessary. Therefore, these will change the power balance of traditional functions in the organization. For this reason, this change must be carefully designed and managed.

## The Right Team Structure

The formation of teams has been a topic of research for decades, and organizations are experimenting with new ways of organizing their teams on a daily basis. Despite many sources and recipes for creating high-performing teams, there are some ground principles, such as *big versus small* and *colocated versus dispersed*, which cannot be underestimated, regardless of the industry or type of product or service you provide.

It is also important to consider that the product and results of work will likely mirror the structure of your team. For example, if you have a geographically dispersed team, product development will tend to be modular, communication will be hard, integration will be a challenge, and quality might drop due to the intrinsic characteristics of your team members. On the other hand, you might gain scale, parallelism, and flexibility. There will be always many trade-offs that the organization needs to evaluate before building or changing team structure.

Despite all of the advancements in technological communication, dispersed teams will always need to deal with issues, including lack of unplanned contact, knowing who to contact about what, the cost of initiating a contact and relationship, the ability to communicate effectively, and lack of trust and transparency (Herbsleb & Grinter, 1999).

Here are some tips for creating the right team structure for your operating model:

- The type of product and value to be delivered should guide the development of your team structure, not the other way around. Remember, the product results are likely to mirror your team structure.

- If you have a geographically dispersed team, assign tasks to different locations according to the best possible architectural separation in a design to be as modular as possible (Herbsleb & Grinter, 1999).

- If you need to split the development, focus on well-understood parts or components in which the plan, relationships, and processes are well identified and as stable as possible (Herbsleb & Grinter, 1999).

- Invest in tools to make it easier to find organizational information, check team availability, and have more effective cross-site meetings, planned and unplanned.

- Avoid multitasking; this will overload the teams and distract them, ultimately impacting their capacity to deal with uncertainties and make fast decisions and solve problems effectively.

- Have the right balance of formal and information communication. It is important to have formal communication channels where everything is registered, captured, and processed; however, do not underestimate the need for informal conversations during coffee and lunch breaks.

- Make information pervasive and visible to everyone on the team. Hiding information or making its access too complex and time consuming is not a good approach to developing a successful operating model.

- Keep your teams small and build a team of teams. Avoid big teams since this will challenge communication and integration. Understand that there are different approaches to organizing teams and getting the right structure for the operating model.

- Adopt a long-lived approach to teams, where members will remain working together for a long period of time. This approach will help improve trust, mutual respect, engagement, a sense of ownership, communication, and team awareness about the work to be done.

## Agile Governance

A successful operating model must adopt an agile governance to ensure we have all of the mechanisms, responsibilities, authority, and indicators, so all decisions are made, coordinated, and steered effectively, to deliver value faster, better, and cheaper.

Governance is a necessary administrative process to ensure results are delivered according to the strategic goals and business purpose. A good practice to designing your agile governance is to adopt a set of key principles. There are several studies and practical examples covering agile governance principles and practices. However, here is a consolidated list of key things you should consider (Luna et al., 2014):

- **Business driven**—it must be guided by the strategy, business priorities, and value. It supports every decision through the governance rituals. It is important that teams develop an accurate sense of the business needs (business awareness) to meet the business targets.
- **Good enough**—there is a saying that perfection is the enemy of *good enough*. Simplicity is the mantra here. Make sure you are not implementing too many processes and checkpoints. Always think about the effectiveness and efficiency of your governance model.
- **People focused**—people must feel they are the most important element of the governance model (and the operating model as well); they need to feel incentivized and recognized; and it is likely they will contribute proactively and creatively to improving the processes and practices continuously.
- **Smart quick wins**—smarter and faster results help build momentum and aggregate impactful outcomes and value over time. Teams should be able to see results frequently but not lose sight of the big prize, so they can feel a sense of accomplishment through the results of their work and contributions.
- **Systematic approach**—teams should be able to handle change naturally and adopt a systematic and adaptive approach to be able to meet business changes and uncertainties.
- **Simple design**—teams should always choose the simpler and feasible solution, balancing agile and lean approaches to get results faster, better, and cheaper. Balance desired results and resource availability—*done* is better than *perfect*.

To illustrate a simple framework for an agile governance, I like to think about three Rs (roles, rituals, and results)—the pillars that cross three main levels: portfolio, program, and teams (Figure 2). For every level, you need to define the key roles; who should be involved; which rituals are needed, at what cadence, duration; and the results we should expect. It is implicit that we will need technology, KPIs, and processes to ensure an agile governance model works properly.

Using the list of principles above and the 3Rs and three levels (portfolio, program, and team), this simple framework is a good start to designing and implementing a successful agile governance model. Leaders need to ensure the right governance process is in place, so the operating model is consistent and aligned with business goals and purpose.

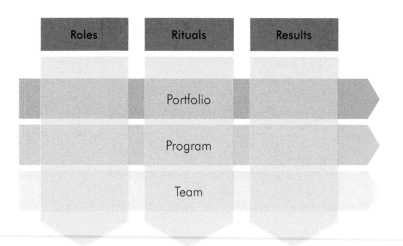

**Figure 2**. Governance levels and the 3Rs key components.

## A Culture of Autonomy

The final characteristic of a successful operating model, but no less important, is to build a culture of autonomy. Why? In a successful operating model, we trust the people we hired to do their best. We need to create a safe environment to openly discuss issues, take risks, and make decisions. This will help the organization become more innovative, effective, and prepared for a perpetual transformation state.

The work of Daniel Pink (2011) on motivation has highlighted the need for autonomy as an integral element of successful and more engaged people. He argues that people want to control what they do. Autonomy also has a positive side effect: it motivates people to think creatively in the face of constraints and crises.

Of course, it is not that simple. To develop team autonomy, we need more. Based on my experience you need, at a minimum, these three principles to create a culture of autonomy as part of your operating model:

- **Value over output.** Measuring outputs instead of value is the first mistake many organizations make when building an operating model. For example, it is a mistake to believe that by measuring hours worked, the company will get better results and return on investment just because you can see where the money is being spent or the hours are allocated. You cannot realistically measure the value or business benefits of a good idea or a good solution by just using hours. Instead, try to understand and see how your teams have contributed to core business goals, such as innovation, sustainability, customer satisfaction, and how these have contributed to grow the business.

- **Context over control.** Do not try to micromanage the work to be done and avoid the temptation to control all decisions across all levels. This is called *unnecessary bureaucracy*. I have a saying here: the more you want to control others, the less likely it will be for them to be creative and innovative in bringing you solutions to problems. Instead, try to ensure there is a clear understanding about the goals, challenges, and risks (high alignment, the vision) and leave the rest to your teams. This is one of the key success factors of the Netflix operating model (Conforto et al., 2018).

- **Give permission to fail.** This one is intrinsically connected with the two other principles. Try to enable and motivate your people to make decisions and learn from their mistakes (Conforto et al., 2019). I know this is not easy, but it is the best way to incentivize a culture of autonomy in the organization and your operating model. From having new ideas to solving problems, to operate in a more efficient way, this must permeate all aspects of work, otherwise, it will not be effective. Failure is not a necessary evil and might not be an evil at all. It is a necessary consequence of doing something new, argues Ed Catmull, coauthor of *Creativity Inc.* (Catmull & Wallace, 2014). A resilient operating model implies a tolerance to fail fast and learn fast.

Successful agile organizations have invested over the years building an operating model that meets their strategic needs and transformation challenges. I have discussed just four of the main characteristics I usually find in successful agile organizations that are demonstrating resiliency. We know that developing an operating model is a journey, not a sprint. So, if this is not a strategic objective for your organization, your executive leadership and teams will not be able to dedicate time and resources to making it happen.

Every successful agile organization has an operating model that is modern, effective, and aligned with their strategy and goals. In these organizations, the operating model is continuously improved and challenged every time there is a sign of misalignment with the company's strategy and North Star.

## References

Accenture Research. (2022). *The resilient operating model.* https://www. accenture.com/us-en/insights/strategy/resilient-operating-model

Catmull, E., & Wallace, A. (2014). *Creativity, Inc: Overcoming the unseen forces that stand in the way of true inspiration.* Random House.

Conforto, E. C., Amaral, D. C., da Silva, S. L., Di Felippo, A., & Kamikawachi, D. S. L. (2016). The agility construct on project management theory. *International Journal of Project Management, 34*(4), 660–674.

Conforto, E. C., & Mendes, J. (2022). Thriving in a persistent transformation context. In *Perpetual transformation: Practical tools, inspiration and best practice to constantly transform your world* (pp. 21–32). Project Management Institute.

Conforto E. C., Vargas, R. V., & Oumarou, T. A. (2018). Strategic agility, the Netflix way. In *World Finance* (pp. 184–185).

Conforto E. C., Vargas, R. V., & Oumarou, T. A. (2019). Making failure work. *The European Business Review.* https://www.europeanbusinessreview.com/making-failure-work/

Gartner. (2022). *Operating model definition. Gartner Glossary.* gartner.com/en/information-technology/glossary/operating-model

Herbsleb, J. D., & Grinter, R. E. (1999). Splitting the organization and integrating the code: Conway's law revisited. In *Proceedings of the 21st*

*International Conference on Software Engineering* (pp. 85–95).

Hines, P., Rich, N., Bicheno, J., Brunt, D., Taylor, D., Butterworth, C., & Sullivan, J. (1998). Value stream management. *International Journal of Logistics Management*, 9(1), 25–42.

Luna, A. J. D. O., Kruchten, P., Pedrosa, M. L. D. E., Neto, H. R., & de Moura, H. P. (2014). State of the art of agile governance: A systematic review. *International Journal of Computer Science and Information Technology*, 6(5), 121–141.

Pink, D. H. (2011). *Drive: The surprising truth about what motivates us.* Penguin.

Womack, J. P., & Jones, D. T. (1996). *Lean thinking: Banish waste and create wealth in your corporation* (p. 37). Simon & Schuster.

## About the Author

**Edivandro Carlos Conforto, PhD,** is a managing director executive and the Latin America lead of the Business Agility and Transformation Practice at Accenture. The author of a number of books and over 50 articles published in business magazines globally, he is a world-renowned and award-winning specialist with over 16 years of experience working with executives in different industry sectors in Brazil, EUA, and Europe. Between 2013 and 2015, he lived in Boston, Massachusetts, USA, where he attended a postdoctoral program at MIT focused on business agility. He holds a PhD and a master's degree in agile management and innovation from the University of São Paulo. He is the first Brazilian to receive international recognition as a result of his contributions to agile management and business agility.

# Why Resilient Organizations Need Generative Leaders

JULIA DHAR, KRISTY ELLMER,
JIM HEMERLING, BRITTANY HEFLIN,
JENS JAHN, AND FANNY POTIER

6

Today, more than ever, we are relying on our leaders to deliver. We're asking more of them than we have in decades.

Put yourself in the shoes of a business leader; or, if you happen to be one, keep those shoes on. Here are some of the daunting priorities and concerns likely to occupy your mind every day:

- Short-term results
- The Great Resignation
- Employee safety and mental health
- Artificial Intelligence (AI)
- Shrinking competitive advantage
- Geopolitical risk
- Always-on transformation
- Increasing complexity
- Ecosystem collaboration
- Customer journeys
- Responding to crises
- Supply chain issues
- Technology and digital revolution
- Polarized communities
- Climate and environmental footprint

Each of these issues is complex and high stakes. Leaders are grappling with this long list and considering how they can build resilient organizations to not only survive but thrive in this future state.

But here is some good news. We ran a year-long research project to examine how business leaders are currently performing and what people want and expect from them. Notably, 75% of the 9,000 employees who responded to our survey said they were satisfied with how leaders performed during the first wave of the COVID-19 pandemic.[1] During that uncertain and frightening time, leaders *did* rise to the occasion. They were creative, flexible, and resilient because they had to be.

## Generative Leadership

Our research suggests that what worked during the pandemic can form the basis for an approach to building and leading resilient organizations, which we call *generative leadership*.

Generative leaders strive to leave the world a better place than they found it. With so much at stake, they are seizing a rare opportunity to do better not just for their shareholders, but also for their customers, teams, society, and the planet. Shareholders are of course vital stakeholders because, as one client told us: "You don't get to have a long term without a short term." But shareholders sit alongside a set of other stakeholders whom generative leaders view as vital to the future. Generative leaders believe that their obligation to society is at the core of their businesses, not just an afterthought.

Many leaders labor under the false impression that there must be a trade-off between doing good for society and the planet and delivering returns to shareholders. But studies consistently show a strong positive correlation between companies' commitment to environmental, societal, and governance (ESG) concerns and financial performance. And this outperformance grows over time—by as much as 40%, according to one study.

This notion of trade-offs shows up especially when leaders are trying to build resilient organizations. One common assumption holds that, to be resilient, a leader and an organization must focus on survival, recovery, and defense, at the expense of bold bets toward innovation and growth. Generative leaders, however, do not recognize this trade-off. On the contrary, they believe that a focus on innovation and growth is necessary to make the organization resilient and adaptive.

Consider IKEA's leadership team, for example. IKEA has a long history of steady and profitable business, but its leaders have never rested on past successes. In 2011, when they decided to fundamentally change their company's relationship with the environment and society, they took immediate and concrete measures. The company started to carefully measure and report on its carbon emissions and those of its thousands of suppliers, and rolled out stringent ethical and sustainable sourcing policies. Once IKEA's leaders had a better view of the company's entire supply chain, they set goals to keep improving over time. They linked those goals to their own annual bonuses and made sustainability a critical criterion in every new business case. And, importantly, they made all these changes while continuing to deliver steady returns to their shareholders.

The generative approach comprises three interconnected elements. First, generative leaders look to reimagine and reinvent their businesses. They think expansively about the future they want to create and focus on the right strategic priorities to reach it. Second, generative leaders create an inspiring and enriching human experience for their people—including outside of work. They lead with purpose and work to inspire and empower people at all levels of the organization. Third, generative leaders find ways to execute and innovate through supercharged teams that work with agility across boundaries. They align their people effectively around the work to be done.

In other words, generative leaders lead equally with their head, heart, and hands. While these are distinct elements of leadership, they come together to reinforce one another (Figure 1). Our data show that organizations unlock the greatest value when these three complementary elements are working together in balance. But it's rare to find an organization whose leadership team excels at leading with all of them. It requires self-awareness and humility and a hunger to keep growing and improving. Let's examine what generative leadership looks like in practice.

**Head** | Reimagining and reinventing the business to serve all stakeholders

Vision
- Be bold yet sustainable; define and seize opportunities to solve big global problems
- Find partners to help your organization do more
- Make big bets on new technology

Transparency
- Be clear, open, and fact-based all the way to the frontline; listen across the organization

Prioritization
- Streamline and simplify big goals so everyone can easily align behind them

Stakeholder inclusion
- Insist on having and hearing diverse voices and balance impact on all stakeholders

Reflection
- Deliberately pause and intentionally entertain opposing views before acting

Creativity
- Foster and reward imagination

**Heart** | Inspiring and enriching the human experience

Purpose-driven
- Foster people's sense of belonging to something bigger than themselves

Recognition
- Inspire people to believe they can do the remarkable and that their contribution matters

Care
- Connect deeply, empathize, and give without expectation

Empathetic listening
- Be present and listen without an agenda

People coaching and development
- Coach and provide feedback to help others discover and realize their potential

Celebration
- Celebrate success and progress rather than perfection

**Hands** | Executing and innovating through supercharged teams

Super-teaming
- Align people across and beyond your organization; use technology to enable them
- Enlist the right technology so that people can focus on doing the things that only humans can do

Resilience
- Adapt as you go; make space for recharge and recovery

People empowerment
- Cede decision-making as much as you can

Courage
- Make and own the tough decisions, sometimes in the absence of consensus

Role modeling
- Help solve problem; be open, curious, and humble; seek out and act on feedback

Experimentation
- Cultivate learning from risk-taking and trial and error

**Figure 1.** The elements of generative leadership.
Sources: BCG and BVA Group leadership survey, October 2020 and July 2021; BCG analysis

## The Head: Reimagining and Reinventing the Business To Serve All Stakeholders

Generative leaders have bold visions for the future. They seek to reimagine and reinvent their businesses for the benefit of all stakeholders. For a generative leadership team, ESG is not a token gesture subordinate to the core business. Sustainable practices are essential to how the business makes money and builds customer and employee loyalty.

Generative leaders not only reimagine their own company's products and services. They lead the way across organizations to reinvent their industries. They cultivate and reward creative thinking in their teams. They pursue new technologies and realize ideas that once seemed impossible.

Enel Group, an Italian energy utility, is a powerful example of what can happen when leaders take a generative approach. Francesco Starace became CEO of Enel in 2014. When he and his leadership team decided to move their conventional industry into renewable energy, they made some remarkably bold and transformational bets over the course of six years:

- They invested in 1,000 startups after reviewing more than 16,000 ideas and pitches.
- They encouraged team members to spend 20% of their time on innovative projects in order to build a culture of innovation and sustainability.
- They introduced a *my best failure* initiative to promote creativity and encourage team members to take risks.
- They rolled out a crowdsourcing platform that allowed outsiders to propose solutions to different innovation challenges; the platform now includes 500,000 participants from more than 100 countries.

To implement these initiatives, Enel reinvented its approach to leadership. It advocates and celebrates *team* leadership, not heroic individual leaders. In 2021, Guido Stratta, Enel's Head of People and Organization, published an essay on soft leadership, writing: "We will move from 'me' to 'we.' This leadership model," he continued, "is attentive to relationships, trust, and respect for each person's talents, while continuing to focus on achieving objectives."

Six years after it began this program of reinvention, Enel became the world's largest supplier of renewable energy. Its bold and creative vision paid off handsomely for shareholders: In those six years, Enel increased its market value by 2.6 times. Enel is a striking example of a generative leadership team that built a resilient organization—an organization that has survived and thrived in an ever-changing context.

## The Heart: Inspiring and Enriching the Human Experience

Generative leaders seek to inspire and enrich the human experience by building great workplaces where people can do their best work and cultivate an adaptive and resilient culture. Employees value recognition and a sense of belonging and a clear purpose that is bigger than themselves. In fact, in our survey, the top four qualities that employees said they seek in their leaders relate to the heart (Figure 2).

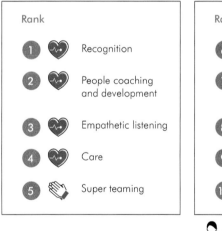

**Figure 2.** The leadership qualities that employees value most.

Sources: BCG and BVA Group leadership survey, October 2020 and July 2021; BCG analysis

Generative leaders achieve these goals by investing in relationships with people. They're empathetic and give of themselves without any expectations, especially during difficult times. Rather than standing apart, they engage with their teams. They prioritize coaching and development to help people realize their full potential. And they champion upskilling and reskilling so people can meet the demands of always-on transformation. They also insist on celebrating success, learning, and progress, not perfection.

Best Buy has done exceptionally well in the heart dimension of leadership. Under former CEO Hubert Joly, the company undertook a successful turnaround that emphasized the employee experience, while its stock generated annual returns of around 20%. "Everybody was saying, 'You better cut, cut, cut, close stores, fire a lot of people,'" Joly told *Harvard Business Review* in 2021.

The usual recipe of turnarounds. No, it started with listening to the frontliners. They had all of the answers. And I spent my first week in a store in St. Cloud (Minnesota) with my blue shirt and my khaki pants, the badge called 'CEO in Training,' to just listen to the frontliners.

"Head count reduction is the last resort," Joly said. Rather than increasing value by extracting personnel costs, Joly and his leadership team pushed to find generative solutions.

Everybody wants to do something good to other people and see how it connects to their work. Create an environment that's very human. Where there's genuine human connection. Where you can focus on creating the environment where they can become the best, biggest, most beautiful version of themselves.

However, improving the human experience is where leaders are most likely to fall short. Our work with clients undergoing major transformations suggests that leaders devote the least amount of time and energy to those qualities (Figure 3).

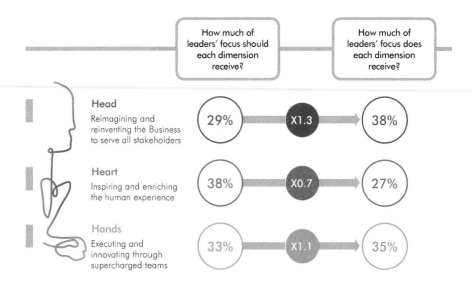

**Figure 3.** Leaders fall short on the heart dimension of leadership.

Sources: BCG and BVA Group leadership survey, October 2020 and July 2021; BCG analysis

## The Hands: Executing and Innovating Through Supercharged Teams

Generative leaders reimagine leadership as a team sport. It's no longer possible, if it ever was, for the hero CEO to grapple alone with the complexity of our constantly and exponentially changing world. Instead, generative leadership calls on leaders to form teams of people with different perspectives within and across organizations, ensuring they don't neglect a key voice or stakeholder. They create high-functioning, empowered, cross-functional *supercharged* teams that execute and innovate with agility. These teams can move quickly and in unison, anticipating where the ball will land rather than focusing on where it is today. They adapt to changing conditions. Their members' primary allegiance is to the team, not to whichever part of their organization they come from. This shift from a me sport to a we sport is a vital characteristic of resilient organizations.

Generative leaders build these teams and organizations in several ways. They engage directly with team members, showing up at team events and on video calls and other occasions. They even work on the frontline, as Joly did, to see things from the bottom up.

Generative leaders ensure that teams work together in the service of the overall purpose and strategy, so that the organization functions as a single entity with everyone working in unison to thrive for the long term. They empower their teams in decision-making and take responsibility for the outcomes. They have the courage to make and own tough decisions, sometimes in the absence of consensus. They encourage learning through experimentation and reward risk taking and continuous improvement.

Generative leaders also seek to be role models; they are open, curious, vulnerable, humble, and they seek out and act on feedback. Role modeling is key to building resilient organizations, leading to a 1.5 times higher success rate during transformation.[2]

Most importantly, generative leaders embrace ecosystems of partners within and outside their own industry, especially those that augment artificial intelligence (AI) and other digital capabilities. These ecosystems require leaders to exert influence over people outside of their direct control. For many leaders, this may mean developing a new skill.

Pfizer leveraged their organizational alignment and became an example of executing and innovating at lightning speed as a united team. In early 2020, Pfizer began a company-wide push to produce a vaccine against COVID-19.

They formed a supercharged team with Germany's BioNTech, a specialist in the development of mRNA vaccines, and a network of academic experts. Mikael Dolsten, MD, PhD, Chief Scientific Officer and President, Worldwide Research, Development and Medical Officer Pfizer, Inc., told us that employees were galvanized to solve this pressing global problem. "Everyone felt that an individual person could make a big contribution to the team effort," he said. Dolsten credits Chief Executive Officer and Chairman Dr. Albert Bourla with rallying the entire team to do what had never been done before. The sense of shared purpose broke down silos. Pfizer became "an unstoppable team," he said. "We needed R&D, manufacturing, everybody to perform at the highest possible level."

To reach this goal, Pfizer created multidisciplinary teams among R&D, manufacturing, and other parts of the business. It also inverted the traditional project time line, imposing a deadline of eight months instead of determining the time line by working backward from each step in the process. Each step was allocated a time slot within those eight months. Serial processes became parallel whenever possible. These measures allowed Pfizer to have its vaccine available by winter in the northern hemisphere. It's hard to overstate how ambitious the eight-month deadline was. Dolsten estimated that such a development process would typically take seven or eight years. But Pfizer's teams "didn't want to let other teams down."

As we now know, Pfizer succeeded in partnership with their collaborators. By the end of 2021, they had delivered more than one billion vaccine doses globally. The ability to confront such a monumental and seemingly impossible challenge, and then rise collectively to meet the moment is an inspiring example of building a resilient organization with generative leaders who lead equally with the head, heart, and hands.

## Putting Generative Leadership Into Practice

Of course, leadership teams can't wait for a global pandemic to help them break down silos and form teams of champions. What are leaders to do? Are they all in a position to reinvent their businesses, enrich the human experience of their employees, and execute and innovate through supercharged teams? If they're not close to practicing generative leadership today, how do they get closer?

As stated earlier, generative leadership is a team sport. It can't be pursued in isolation. An organization that relies on one person for direction, energy, and inspiration is inherently brittle. It can fail if a single link in the chain breaks. A resilient organization is one that builds connected systems and shares the load, so that no one link in the chain is strained more than it can bear. Enabling the organization in this way can lead to a 1.7 times higher success rate in transformations.[3] Building interconnected teams in this way requires trust and connection across the organization, as well as continual feedback, reflection, and coaching. The path will be different for different leadership teams, because no two teams will have identical starting points or needs.

Becoming more generative is a long-term pursuit. Like healthy living or athletic conditioning, it requires fundamental and permanent lifestyle changes rather than episodic training or dieting.

Whether you are already on the journey or just getting started, the following practices can help leaders and leadership teams become more generative. These practices will help clarify the mission of a leader and team by focusing on the head, the heart, and the hands of leadership.

## Head. To help further develop these capabilities:

- Ask yourself and the members of your team: What would your organization need to do to reinvent itself to thrive in the complex and ever-changing context of today and our future? Imagine a future in which you do not survive. What could you have done differently?
- Set up a monthly sounding-board session with select customers, suppliers, employees, and societal stakeholders to solicit suggestions on how to further improve your business while having a positive environmental and social impact.

## Heart. To help further develop this skill:

- Spend at least a few days each quarter with frontline employees in order to understand their daily work and listen to their concerns. It's not enough to shake hands or appear on occasional video calls with the team. *Being present* means more than meeting and greeting team members. It means spending enough time with them to understand their ideas about how things might be improved and where they need your help. Or take it a step further and participate in their daily activities at work alongside them.
- Block out one hour a week to check in one-on-one with team members—junior people, peers, or partners—about how they and their families are doing and how they feel about their work. Throw away the agenda and listen; these conversations build heart.

**Hands. To help further develop supercharged teams and other capabilities:**

- Ask yourself which of your priorities could be better achieved by increasing cross-functional teams both inside and outside of your organization. Where do you need more people working across current team boundaries? How can you help them to do so?
- Invite a different set of team members monthly to provide feedback on how they can better leverage technology to supercharge their work. Do your team members have the right set and amount of data to make informed decisions? Are their technological tools helping or hindering their ability to create supercharged teams?

Throughout the world, we are starting to see generative leadership teams emerge. These teams are pursuing a better vision for the workplace, society, and our planet. Their view of the future is bright and optimistic, and they are committing their companies to renewing Earth's depleted resources. In this moment of tremendous and accelerating change, the world is calling for leaders who can stand up and make a lasting difference. Generative leaders are answering the call.

### Acknowledgments

The authors would like to thank the following colleagues for their valuable contributions to the development of this article: Cailin Ahern, Vikram Bhalla, Jean-Michel Caye, Divya Chanana, Wanjun Fang, Grant Freeland, Bill Higgins, Marie Humblot-Ferrero, Philippine Leccia, Debbie Lovich, Mickey McManus, and Robert Werner.

### Footnotes

1   This survey was conducted in France, Germany, Spain, and the United Kingdom by BVA Group in October 2020; it was conducted in Brazil, Chile, China, India, and the United States in July 2021.

2   BCG Transformation Check.

3   Ibid.

## About the Authors

**Julia Dhar** is a Managing Director & Partner at BCG. She leads *BeSmart, BCG's Behavioral Economics and Behavioral Insights initiative*. Trained as a behavioral economist, Julia champions the use of behavioral insights to improve product and service design and delivery across the organizations in the public and private sectors.

**Kristy Ellmer** is a Managing Director & Partner at BCG, and the Global Leader of BCG's Change & Culture Offer within the People and Organization Practice. Kristy is an experienced transformation leader with over 15 years of leading large-scale, holistic programs.

**Jim Hemerling** is a Managing Director & Senior Partner at BCG. He is a leader in BCG's People and Organization and Transformation practices and leads the Leadership topic globally. With over 30 years of experience as a senior advisor, Jim has widespread experience cultivating high-performing cultures to enable holistic, sustainable performance in organizations.

**Brittany Heflin** serves as the Global Leadership and Coaching Offer Manager within BCG's People and Organization practice. She is a certified executive coach and has over a decade of experience as an organizational effectiveness consultant with rich experience in culture, change management, and leadership.

**Jens Jahn** is a Managing Director & Partner at BCG. He is a core member of BCG's People and Organization and Operations practice areas. He is an expert and leader in the people side of transformations and turnarounds, post merger integrations, reorganizations, and restructurings.

**Fanny Potier** is a Partner & Associate Director at BCG within the People and Organization practice. She is a certified coach and global expert in talent and leadership topics with broad industry focus. She has a breadth of experience in organizational design, post merger integration, transformation, and workforce restructuring, and human resources.

# Putting Your Organization on the Performance Curve to Support Agility and Resilience

VANESSA DIETZEL AND LAURA WATKINS

7

If the people in your organization are not personally agile and resilient in the face of external challenges and change, then it will make little difference whether you have an adaptable strategy, agile approaches, and great collaboration tools. And we can lose our footing quickly, perhaps without realizing. Our client Rachel was a confident CEO entrepreneur of a fast-growing business. When her industry was disrupted by a new entrant, she became increasingly defensive, making decisions reactively, and struggling to talk openly with her colleagues. She and her team were tense, stuck, and making piecemeal changes, just when they most needed to bring quality thinking to adapt their strategy.

Over the past two years we have faced enormous change and uncertainty, and this level of challenge looks set to continue. How can we bring our best in moments of adversity and use them to build our agility and resilience for the future? To do this, organizations need cultures that support all of their people to grow their ability to adapt. This is not simply about acquiring new knowledge or skills, but also about strengthening the human capacity to deal with complexity, challenge, and change. We call this deeper, personal growth *being on the performance curve*. In a performance curve culture, people challenge and support one another to grow in this way.

When we grow deeply, we are evolving the complex brain wiring that guides how we function in the world. We call this our *inner operating system*. Often outside our awareness, it determines how we make sense of situations, prioritize what matters, react emotionally, and take action. The more we can become aware of the mindsets, emotional responses, and habits that drive us, the more we can take charge of them to better deal with challenges, change, and complexity. For example, when Rachel understood the mindsets that led her to feeling defensive, she was able to adapt how she thought and responded, and to function better under pressure.

How people grow and perform at this deeper, more personal level, is crucial to both individual and collective success. Yet we've seen few organizations with a culture that supports people working on their inner operating system as part of their normal day job. Cultures where, instead of sending people to coaching, training courses, or therapists, the inner growth is an integral part of the work of managers, colleagues, and teams. It is time for organizations to evolve from what we see as *short-term delivery cultures* (STDC) to *performance curve cultures*, to better tackle the challenges of our times. In this article, we will bring alive what a performance curve culture looks like and the practical steps you can take to strengthen yours (Table 1).

Table 1. Defining Characteristics of a Short-Term Delivery Culture (STDC) and a Performance Curve Culture

| | Short-Term Delivery Culture | Performance Curve Culture |
|---|---|---|
| Behaviors | • We are laser-focused on **getting things done**, often at the expense of development.<br>• We teach people **skills** and **guide their behaviors**. | • We use **development to get work done faster and better**.<br>• We help people develop their **mindsets**, as well as skills and behaviors. |
| Mindsets | • People need to **prove themselves** when facing challenges (fixed mindset).<br>• It's **hard** to get results and develop people.<br>• It's **not safe to discuss mindsets**.<br>• Learning happens in **courses or ad hoc**, influenced by an **annual review**. | • Challenging situations are **opportunities to grow** (growth mindset).<br>• Developing people **helps get results**.<br>• It's **helpful to discuss mindsets**.<br>• Everyone can **learn every day**, supported by regular feedback and training. |
| Outcomes | • People grow mostly **on the surface (skills, some behaviors)**.<br>• People put on their **best performance** today, with less focus on building future capacity.<br>• We get things **done the usual way, right away**. | • People grow at **all levels of the inner operating system** (i.e., mindsets, emotions, behaviors).<br>• Today's delivery builds **long-term capacity**.<br>• Sometimes we **slow down to speed up** or find new approaches. |

## Expanding From Short-Term Delivery Cultures to Performance Curve Cultures

Let's compare these two cultures, looking at behaviors, underlying mindsets, and outcomes. In an STDC, we are single minded about getting results via the most direct route. For example, if we have a job to be done, we ask the most skilled team member. We give people the tools and skills to do the job at hand, along with guiding their behaviors to complete the task. By contrast, in a performance curve culture, we always ask how we can use development to get work done faster and better. We see development versus delivery as a paradox that can be unlocked, not an either/or choice. For example, we might match the most skilled team member to mentor the next most skilled member. We also focus on the growth of people's inner operating systems (mindsets, emotions, habits) as well as skills and behaviors.

In STDCs, we often see a fixed mindset; in other words, people believe that our capability is innate and fixed, and so challenges are a chance to prove ourselves. In performance curve cultures we usually see more of a growth mindset; in other words, we believe that our or others' capabilities can grow, so a challenge is a chance to stretch ourselves and develop.

This distinction is key, because a fixed mindset is more likely to encourage our brain into a fight-flight-or-freeze response, what we call *protect mode*. We react quickly and automatically, rather than taking time to make deliberate, proactive choices about the best response in a given situation. It is like an autopilot with a limited range of emergency functions, as our client Rachel experienced. It keeps us safe when facing immediate physical danger, such as a tiger in the jungle, but it decreases activity in many parts of the executive center of the brain's prefrontal cortex. This reduces our ability to regulate our emotions, bring our best thinking to problems, and relate skillfully to others. It caps our effectiveness and limits what we can achieve when faced with the often complex challenges of modern life. And, if protect mode becomes our habitual way of operating instead of an occasional emergency response, we increasingly erode the well-being and functioning of our bodies and minds.

By contrast, a growth mindset is more likely to help our brains be in *explore mode*, where our brain is firing on all cylinders to pursue opportunities and rewards. We can do the complex work of manipulating information in our heads, creating options, exploring perspectives, empathizing, and thinking through decisions. We can bring more creativity and intuition to tackle difficult issues and collaborate better with others, all of which also increase our well-being and make us emotionally more resilient. This mindset helps people open up, enabling them to work on their inner operating systems together. By contrast, in an STDC, it feels unsafe to openly discuss mindsets.

STDCs typically rely on annual review processes and training to drive the learning process. Performance curve cultures place attention on learning 365 days a year. Development happens in the middle of our regular work, to help our work go faster and better, not as a separate activity. And learning is for everyone, not just the high potentials or senior leaders.

Accordingly, people develop more narrowly in STDCs. They may be more compliant and reliable today, but this command-and-control management does nothing to support agility in our complex and changing world. Performance curve cultures build capacity for the long term. We may feel we are slowing down slightly—for example, to give a person a chance to try something—or they may bring a different approach. But this will, over time, result in speed and agility.

Performance curve cultures are not a soft and fluffy human resource (HR) initiative. These environments feel supportive but not cozy, as we are asked to become aware of, and continually adapt, our inner operating system; including deep-seated beliefs that have shaped our sense of identity. We learn to overcome problems better, anticipate more, take more risks, and make better decisions, all at greater pace. This drives business results, develops and retains our people, and leads to long-term business performance. It's a source of competitive advantage, but it also requires a fundamentally different type of leadership.

## How Can Leaders Build a Performance Curve Culture?

While most of us know how much our inner operating systems influence our effectiveness, most on-the-job coaching is about technical skills and deliverables. It is often seen as taboo to talk about our mindsets and emotions: a sign of weakness, risky, or just not done in the national or company culture. Leaders can unblock that taboo through role modeling. If leaders show that they are open to personal growth, it helps people see that, rather than hiding potential weaknesses in our inner operating system (from ourselves or others), they can learn faster by talking about them. It might feel uncomfortable initially, but you will give others permission to do the same.

In parallel, we have found success comes from infusing developmental habits into four central organizational elements, which we will cover in turn here. For each element, we will share examples of habits you could build into teams' ways of working. There is no single recipe for cultivating a performance curve culture: choose what will work for your context.

## Building Teams and Assigning Work

The team setup provides the environment for individual and collective development. Are team members comfortable expressing vulnerability because this is met with empathy? Do they challenge one another's thinking daily? We can create a fertile environment by paying careful attention to who works with whom, how the work is allocated, and how teamwork begins and ends. Here are some ideas:

- **Make sure everyone has a challenging assignment.** Give people assignments that force them to see things from fresh angles, build new skills, or integrate multiple perspectives. Even small reassignments can trigger such learning. One of the CEOs we interviewed for our book, *The Performance Curve*, highlighted how important it is to come up with these creative ways of challenging people in smaller organizations like his own, where there are fewer opportunities for doing so by moving them through different roles.

- **Support the challenge.** High challenge should be accompanied by good support, so individuals learn required new skills but also ensure their inner operating system sets them up to succeed, for example, avoiding succumbing to *protect mode*. Pairing people, for example, one more experienced with one less experienced team member, is an age-old technique for transferring skills. However, you can set up pairs to specifically help people do inner operating system work together, for example, by observing each other at work, or talking through their challenges and asking each other questions.

- **Launch the team with developmental interactions.** Ideally, this would include some individual sharing and some collective exchange, which builds an open flow of empathy and vulnerability and provides structure for inner operating system growth. Individuals might share their development goals or what drives them toward the protect and explore modes. The collective exchange could be anything that involves practicing talking about inner operating systems together, so that people are able to do this later when they are under pressure. For example, premortems: the team imagines themselves in the future and looks back to brainstorm risks and success factors.

- Ensure your team has **regular check-ins and postmortems**, which include talking about how the team's inner operating systems are helping and hindering performance. For example, when identifying lessons learned and what to do differently, talk about how to adjust mindsets and habits, or how to help each other get back into the explore mode when under pressure. Early in the COVID-19 pandemic, we ran check-ins for dozens of country leadership teams at one organization. Although most teams felt the pandemic brought them closer together, these sessions acted as a pressure valve, made it normal to talk about mindsets and emotions, and set the teams up for the difficult winter ahead. Using a facilitator helps, but it doesn't need to be an external coach and you can train people to do this for one another's teams.

## Holding Meetings

How much of your working time do you spend in meetings? Participants in our leadership programs typically say around 80%. That's a lot of time. So what can we do in meetings to help people bring their best and develop agility and resilience? For example, we might support people to be in explore mode or to think in more complex ways. Here are some ideas, each of which might take a few minutes to set up but will pay back in development, discussion quality, and team cohesion:

- **Send invites and allocate roles with development in mind.** Another CEO we profile in *The Performance Curve* regularly invites leaders to bring their team to meetings with him, rather than come alone. This allows him to expand people's thinking, reinforce company priorities and values, and encourage productive mindsets. Once at the meeting, you can also allocate roles to support development. Rotating who chairs the team meeting pushes people to integrate different perspectives and bring bigger-picture thinking. One of our clients invites her junior team members to lead part of the meeting; they find this very motivating, putting a lot of thought into how to make their slot impactful.
- **Start the meeting with a shared practice** that gets everyone ready to bring their best, to settle protect mode and encourage explore mode. You could run a short mindfulness practice, simply allow a couple of minutes of quiet, or invite each person to share something they are grateful for. You could also prime people to bring their best by asking them to set an intention for a quality they will bring to the meeting (e.g., curiosity, persistence) or how they will contribute (e.g., ask questions, be kindly challenging).
- **Infuse a sense of purpose into the meeting.** Bringing purpose into the meeting helps people keep the bigger picture in mind, take the focus off themselves and their needs, and encourage better quality thinking. This could be as simple as starting a meeting with a recent customer success or inviting team members to share what is on their customers' worry lists.

- **Ask questions** that help people get perspective on, and be more versatile with, their thinking. What sorts of questions can help accomplish this? We can use questions that reinforce helpful mindsets, such as: In what ways might we have contributed more to this situation than we realize? (accountability mindset) Or, if we consider all of the different needs, what might we do? (big picture mindset). We can also use questions to unlock paradoxes, such as: What is really at the heart of this dilemma? Or, how could doing X actually get us more of Y?

## Encourage Feedback Plus Questions

Frequent, informal feedback supports people to grow sustainably every day, especially when it is combined with questions that trigger insight into our inner operating systems. We believe feedback should be so woven into ways of interacting that people rarely see feedback discussions as something distinct. Here are some ideas to move in that direction:

- **Inspire people with a positive vision of the culture you are seeking to create.** Make clear the benefits to them and others. Call your culture something positive, such as a *development culture*, rather than a *feedback culture*. Feedback is just a means to this end, and the very term sends many people into protect mode.

- **Make it routine that everyone knows what everyone else is working on.** This helps people help each other and also encourages a growth mindset, because it shows everyone is a work in progress. You could get everyone to share their development goals quarterly or at the start of a project. Or you could go one step further and put up a poster on which everyone writes their current development goals.

- **Create little moments where feedback flows.** You could hold a feedback discussion in a group, starting with: How effective was this meeting on a scale of 1 to 10? What could we do next time to get to 9 or 10? Or share something someone else said that shifted your thinking. Or you could close a meeting with a quick round of feedback, as a group or in pairs. Encourage people to give feedback on the work product (e.g., "your analysis was clear") and touch on the inner operating system (e.g., "noticed you get quiet when X topic came up but I really felt we could have benefited from your view"). Encourage them to ask coaching questions (e.g., Did you notice that? What were you thinking or feeling when you got quiet?).

- **Create a buddy system.** Many of our clients have implemented buddy systems across organizational boundaries. It is motivating, builds muscles for growing, and accelerates the learning across department lines. Time lost on direct work will be rewarded through the deep learning and stronger relationships. You could pair people up with people from the same team, other departments, or different seniority levels. The key is that the buddies bring empathy and vulnerability, and intertwine feedback and asking questions that encourage their partners to gain insights for their inner operating system.

### Use Training to Cultivate a Performance Curve Culture

In a performance curve culture, training builds the skills needed for developing our inner operating system (as well as technical or interpersonal skills). Training should equip people to create, maintain, and benefit from a performance curve culture; in other words, give them tools and techniques to help them learn deeply and daily, individually and collectively. Consider:

- How many of your learning interventions are delivered in a single event? How could you extend the learning period and help people get brilliant at learning every day, in their regular work settings?
- What percentage of your training budget is spent on helping people work with their inner operating systems versus building skills? How could you make developmental learning a part of every program?
- To what extent do you help new employees understand their inner operating systems, strengthen their growth mindset, and know how to participate in a performance curve culture? How could you do this earlier and better?
- How much do you invest in coaching skills inside the line organization? How could you build basic coaching skills in everyone, including individual contributors?
- How much do your executive team and board work on their ability to model a performance curve culture? If you feel they could do more, what would be the courageous move to make that happen?

## Building Performance Curve Cultures Beyond Work

We have laid out a range of ways for building teams and organizations that support you and others to be agile and resilient when facing challenges and, in doing so, build capacity for the future. Although we have focused primarily on work settings, hopefully this has also inspired some ideas you could try out with friends, family, or community groups. We can make a powerful difference through helping one another develop our inner operating systems. It will boost our individual effectiveness and well-being and help address the collective economic, social, and environmental issues of our times.

## About the Authors

**Vanessa Dietzel** is a leadership coach helping leaders and their organizations achieve top performance in a sustainable, purpose-led way. She started her career with Boston Consulting Group in London and Sydney, and blends her corporate experience with coaching, and teaching breathwork and yoga. She has a BSc in International Relations from London School of Economics and Political Science and has trained in a range of personal and group development techniques.

**Laura Watkins** is a neuroscientist and leadership and organization specialist. She has a PhD in Cognitive Neuroscience from Cambridge University and an MA in Physiology and Psychology from Oxford University. She began her career at McKinsey & Co., where she cofounded their leadership practice in Europe. She founded The Cognitas Group, a leadership and organizational consultancy, and Jumpstart Development, which provides virtual leadership development.

This article is adapted from their book, *The Performance Curve* (Bloomsbury Business, 2021).

# Recruiting, Retaining, and Leading High Performers

RUTH GOTIAN

# The Business Case for Having More High Achievers

Why should anyone strive to be a high achiever? Perhaps the right question is: Why wouldn't one want to achieve more? I study extreme high achievers, including astronauts, Nobel Prize winners, and Olympic champions. Without question, they all strive for a life of significance, where their work can inspire and impact a whole new generation. Sure, the promotions, high salaries, and recognition are great, but for all of these top performers, those were never their motivation. It was neither the Nobel Prize nor Olympic medal that inspired them. Instead, they found purpose in what they did, which led them to love the journey (Gotian, 2022). As shared in the book, *The Success Factor*, the process is as exciting as the result. Frankly, they could not picture themselves doing anything else and strive to leave this world better than they found it. High achievers want to create paradigm shifts in the ways people think, process, and do things. They are constantly innovative in their thinking and execution and have little patience for those who strive for less.

Our current work models do not allow people to perform at their best. We get plenty of lip service, but the models tell a different story. Consider the annual performance appraisals within most organizations; they occur once a year, intending to determine if you are hitting key metrics. Often they are listed on a scale, for example, one to five, with three being average. If you score a three, you are *meeting expectations*. There is no further conversation as predefined, often archaic metrics are successfully achieved. You are told to keep doing what you are doing. You stay entirely under the radar.

If you are a high potential, a four, or a high achiever, a five, you are *exceeding expectations*. With a smile, you are told how grateful the company is that you are part of the team and you might get a bigger bonus, but that is about it. The fact that you are not causing anyone any grief and consistently producing quality work means that you are not someone who is a cause for concern. Just continue with your work. No one asks you any questions or offers you any challenges or resources.

If you fall below a three, you are *not meeting expectations*. These people not meeting baseline requirements cause everyone to pounce into action. If you fail to meet specific metrics, a team of people parachutes down to help the poor performer. The poor performer gets a Performance Improvement Plan (PIP), also known as a Corrective Action Plan (CAP). Metrics are developed, the poor performers are sent to courses and workshops to learn skills to meet said metrics, and a supervisor is assigned to hold them accountable.

These are a lot of resources and time to spend on someone who is a poor performer, and everyone sees this. The high potentials and high achievers observe the lopsided allocation of resources and get annoyed; they view it as poor performance getting rewarded. The high achievers are eager to learn new skills and get sent to courses and workshops, but no one is offering them the same opportunities. As we reimagine work, consider giving those same levels of resources to the top performers.

Ask any leader, and they will tell you they spend 90% of their time on 10% of the employees and these are usually the troublemakers. If you are not on their radar, that means you are not at the bottom of the pool. No news is good news, or is it? If you are not on their radar, you are not getting 90% of their attention. If your organization plans on being innovative, growth oriented, resilient, and adaptive, recruiting and retaining high achievers may be the solution.

High achievers are 400% more productive than an average employee (O'Boyle & Aguinis, 2012; Willyerd, 2014). As such, you would not need as many to do the same level of work. Stock your employee base with high achievers if you want innovative employees who develop next-level ideas. If you do not, the high achievers and likely the high potentials will leave. At best, you are left with average employees. At worst, you will have an employee base of poor performers. Viewing it this way, there is a business case for recruiting, retaining, and leading high performers.

If you want to be the organization known for developing, retaining, and growing top talent, you need to reimagine what you are doing with your high achievers. It is time to shift the pendulum and invest the time and resources in those who routinely outperform and exceed predetermined benchmarks. To start, sometimes, all you need to do is ask the high performers what they need to continuously grow and stay challenged.

## Opportunities for Exposure

When high achievers work on something, they are all in. They want to do their best work and find creative, innovative, and more efficient ways to achieve their goals. If you want to retain and lead these high performers, you need to offer them opportunities for exposure.

## Stretch Assignments

High achievers fear not trying more than they fear failing; however, if they can learn even one new skill, they are eager to try. So offer them stretch assignments, where they can stretch their creative muscles, learn something new, and make new connections. They will tackle the challenge head-on and bring a fresh new perspective, which might be refreshing and alleviate the tired "we've always done it that way" approach, which stifles creativity and innovation.

## Exposure and Visibility

If you want to lead high achievers, put a spotlight on their work and achievements. Bring them into meetings with higher-level leaders and let them showcase their accomplishments. Do not, under any circumstances, present their work for them; instead, pass the leadership baton—also known as *situational leadership*—and put the spotlight on them. After all, they know their work best, and practicing presenting it, not just doing it, is a critical skill to learn. Giving them credit for their work is not just nice, it is the right thing to do.

## Lead Global Teams

To grow in your career, you need to have greater responsibility; typically, this is in the form of budgets or people. The higher ranking the people you manage, the greater your responsibility and reach. If your team is global, the reach is further. Consider having your high achiever lead teams across multiple locations as a developmental and retention plan.

## Give Them Autonomy

High achievers constantly question what would happen *if*, or wonder what would happen if they try something different. As mentioned, they fear not trying more than they fear failing. They never question if they can overcome a challenge because they are confident they will. Instead, they focus on how to overcome the challenge. They ask themselves what is the strategy they had not thought of yet. That last word, *yet*, is critical. It means there will be a great deal of trial and error. If you are to lead high achievers, give them the breathing room to try and fail. They want to succeed more than anyone but need the freedom to ideate.

No one likes to be micromanaged, especially high achievers. They actively think and experiment and need a quiet space to do so. They have no need to report back on every trial and misstep. When they have something to share, they will. Give them space.

## Building Advancement Pathways

If you want to retain your high achievers, understand that they rapidly need promotion opportunities. Do not keep them stagnant just because their boss is stuck in their career. Instead, actively bring opportunities for advancement to their attention and encourage them to apply. Tell them they have your full support. If they are missing a skill, suggest how they can fill the gap. Introduce them to others who can help train them in the needed skill. Constantly suggesting opportunities for advancement sends an undeniable signal that the company invests in high achievers.

## Offer Further Training

High achievers are always connecting dots that others do not see (Gotian, 2022). They constantly scan for information from various sources such as books, articles, webinars, lectures, and conversations with others. They look both within and outside their organization and field. They are always on the hunt for new information, new ideas, and new thought leadership.

Knowing this, initiate a conversation with your high achiever and offer to add to help them learn new things. Consider asking the high achiever what skill they would like to learn. Ask them what course or conference they would like to attend. Do not worry about them missing days of work, as high achievers do not stop working at a fixed time when the workday is nominally over; they work on a job through to completion. They will take the new knowledge they just learned and seek ways to implement it immediately, and the return on investment will be almost immediate.

If you want to go the extra step, consider giving high achievers a professional development allowance that lets them choose their courses.

The high achievers will recognize that you are invested in their success and will feel rejuvenated. As they master new skills, they will stretch their resiliency and loyalty, because this is a challenge they are eager to solve, and quitting is not in their vocabulary.

## Reward Your High Achievers

Remember those group projects in college? There was always that one person who carried the group and got everyone on the same page. And there was another one whose mind would work one million miles a minute; they would shoot out ideas faster than anyone could write them down. Then another person would execute the ideas and write the majority of the paper. Nevertheless, every group project had one person who did nothing more than spell check, not anything close to resembling their fair share of the work, not even close. However, their name appeared on the paper and carried the same weight as yours. It was frustrating then, and it is even more infuriating when it happens in the workplace.

High achievers will not accept this. They do not want to be part of a group that either unfairly dilutes or enhances any one person's achievements. Sure, they wish to be compensated for their work; who doesn't? However, if you ignore their consistent good work and do not differentiate among compensation models within groups, you risk losing your high achievers. Every person in a group has a different function, strength, and worth. Therefore, the high achievers expect a pay model that compensates for individual rather than group performance.

While compensation is necessary, it is not the only critical variable. High achievers want to see examples of innovation, creativity, curiosity, and desire to consistently raise the bar of excellence. Good is never good enough, and the saying *"We have always done it that way"* is akin to nails on the blackboard for high achievers. Ensure that you align recognition with superior performance. Do not recognize a baseline expectation such as arriving on time or keeping a neat workstation. That is a sure-fire way to lose credibility. Instead, focus on ingenuity, innovation, creativity, curiosity, and output.

## Mentor Your High Performers

The research is clear (Eby et al., 2008, Allen et al., 2004). Those who are mentored out earn and outperform those who are not. Mentored individuals have higher productivity, get promoted more often, earn higher salaries, and suffer less burnout than their non mentored counterparts. They are also more loyal to the organization. If you want your employees to be resilient and stretch beyond what they think is possible, surround them with a team of mentors who can offer perspectives, ideas, expertise, and a network they can tap into.

## Copy and Paste is Not a Strategy

If something worked with a different team or organization, copying and pasting the same strategy or program into your team or organization will fall flat and make you lose credibility. Cultures and group dynamics vary among organizations, so what was a resounding success at one institution may fail to launch in another. It is inauthentic and you will be viewed as someone who only knows one plan and puts it on repeat in every organization. Instead, you must respect the history and culture of your current team and institution and find ways to work within that dynamic. Ignoring this and simply repeating past successes with new people will be resented, because you are ignoring the strengths and traditions of your current team members.

## Understanding Adult Learners

To truly be a resilient organization, you must understand the adults who work within it and specifically how they learn. Malcolm Knowles, the grandfather of adult learning, developed these six assumptions about adult learners, the backbone of every leadership and educational development model (Knowles, 1984):

1. Adults prefer to choose how they will learn. It is what is known as self-directed learning. They want to have a voice in their learning goals, and process and develop self-directed learning attributes.
2. We all have experiences that we bring into our learning. Adults want and need to tap into those experiences to ground their learning.
3. An adult's readiness to learn is correlated to their social role. If your job does not expect you to learn and grow, why would you be motivated to be curious?
4. Adults need immediate use of their newly learned knowledge. They want to implement it and see its impact.
5. Adult learners are fueled by intrinsic motivation (Deci et al., 2001). They have a burning desire to learn something new, a fire in their belly. Their learning is maximized when they are not doing it for external rewards such as diplomas, bonuses, or public recognition.
6. When you are dealing with other pressures, such as children or a mortgage, every moment is precious. You need to know why you are learning something. You cannot simply memorize random facts or

impractical tidbits. This is not helpful to adult learners.
Understanding how adults learn will help you create and develop
programs with the user in mind. It is not simply about transferring
knowledge. Doing it correctly will ensure the knowledge is used and
enhanced (Freire, 2000).

## Recruitment

Optimizing and leveraging tools and programs to retain and lead your high
performers is not just a nice thing to do; it is also a great recruitment tool. Look
at the high achievers. Who do you think their friends are? It is simple: they are
other high achievers. When they hear of how the top performers are treated
within your organization, their friends will start talking about it and, in short
order, they will become your best recruiters. However, it does not end there.
Once you get a group of high achievers together and they know, like, and trust
one another, they will start innovating, ideating, and working well together, in a
manner greater than the sum of its parts.

There has been a mass exodus from the workplace, resulting in what is
commonly known as The Great Resignation. The strategies that worked before
will not work now. We have new variables in place, including understanding the
parameters, benefits, and challenges of remote work. Employees are more vocal
about their unwavering desire and need to have greater balance and shorter
commutes in their lives. There is a crisis but also an opportunity. We may not
need the same types of people we employed in the past. Focusing on high
achievers offers an opportunity for more significant innovation and productivity.
There is a real business case for shifting our focus to these top performers.

Information in this article is adapted from the book *The Success Factor:
Developing the Mindset and Skillset for Peak Business Performance*, by Ruth
Gotian (Kogan Page, 2022).

## References

Allen, T., Eby, L., Poteet, M., Lentz, E., & Lima, L. (2004). Career benefits associated with mentoring for protegee: A meta analysis. *Journal of Applied Psychology, 89*(1), 127.

Deci, E. L., Koestner, R., & Ryan, R. M. (2001). Extrinsic rewards and intrinsic motivation in education: Reconsidered once again. *Review of Educational Research, 71*(1), 1–27.

Eby, L. T., Allen, T. D., Evan, S. C., Ng, T., & Dubois, D. (2008). Does mentoring matter? A multidiciplinary meta-analysis comparing mentored and non-mentored individuals. *Journal of Vocational Behavior, 72*(2), 254–267.

Freire, P. (2000). *Pedagogy of the oppressed.* Continuum International Publishing Group.

Gotian, R. (2022). *The success factor: Developing the mindset and skillset for peak business performance.* Kogan Page.

Knowles, M. S. (1984). *The adult learner: A neglected species.* Gulf.

O'Boyle, E. Jr., & Aguinis, H. (2012). The best and the rest: Revisiting the norm of normality of individual performance. *Personnel Psychology, 65*(1), 79–119.

Willyerd, K. (2014). What high performers want at work. *Harvard Business Review.* https://hbr.org/2014/11/what-high-performers-want-at-work

## About the Author

**Ruth Gotian, EdD, MS,** is a social scientist and the Chief Learning Officer and Assistant Professor of Education in Anesthesiology at Weill Cornell Medicine, New York City. She is the author of *The Success Factor* (Kogan-Page, 2022) and winner of the 2021 Thinkers50 Radar Award.

# Organizations as Resilient Living Systems

GUDRUN ERLA JONSDOTTIR AND
BJARNI SNÆBJÖRN JÓNSSON

Nowhere in the world has the word *coronavirus* not been heard. Within just a few weeks in 2020, the word was on everyone's lips. At the time, little did the world know how much the pandemic would change the way we lived. And, just when we seemed to be approaching the end of the COVID-19 pandemic, providing room for rebuilding, yet another crisis erupted with the war in Ukraine, causing disruptive consequences in many parts of the world.

Nobody now doubts the growing pressure on people and organizations around the world to change and cope with what is happening and what is yet to come. In fact, the changes have been transformational. Over the last few years, the world's transformation has been phenomenal. The world shut down; governments, organizations, and people everywhere had to adapt with little preparation and notice. Adapting to the situation went well for some but proved more difficult for others. Focusing on organizations, which, after all, consist of people with a shared culture, the question becomes: How do we build resilient organizations that embrace challenges as opportunities?

## In Every Crisis Lies the Seed of Opportunity

In the Chinese language, the word *crisis* is composed of two characters, one representing danger and the other opportunity. Looking at threats as opportunities, as two sides of the same coin, still applies and is a good reminder of why the way we perceive a given situation is of the essence. Perception can make the distinction between those who survive and those who do not. After all, some of the greatest breakthroughs in human history were accomplished during a crisis. However, to turn a danger or threat into an opportunity, a positive and innovative mindset is required for the organization to be adaptable. As Maya Angelou put it: "If you don't like something, change it. If you can't change it, change your attitude."

For years, leaders have been warned that the operational environment is becoming increasingly volatile, uncertain, complex, and ambiguous (VUCA). In some parts of the world, especially industrialized countries, we have grown accustomed to relative stability since World War II, with the exception of two oil crises. During the last 15 years, however, we have seen one major crisis after another, starting with the financial crisis in 2008, the COVID-19 pandemic in 2020, and now a major war in Ukraine. The advent of the changes these events are causing is indisputable as is the inability to control the situation. What is left, then, is changing the attitude and embracing the opportunities these events could present. This calls for resilience and, with regard to organizations, changing mindsets.

Resilience is defined by *Merriam-Webster Dictionary* as "an ability to recover from or adjust easily to misfortune or change;" therefore, the objective of organizations must be to constantly adapt through resilience. The balance between flexibility and order is essential in building a resilient organization. More than anything else, building resilient organizations is all about leadership, carefully crafting and following through with a cultural evolution that embraces changes and enables the organization to become agile, responding to opportunities and seizing them. It is about planting seeds of positivity to foster opportunities, and not being afraid to make mistakes. To do so, leaders must lead by example. Not doing so creates confusion and chaos. After all, as the mind controls the body, so does culture control organizations.

## Resilient Organizational Culture

Organizations are living systems; they are born, go through life cycle stages, mature, age, and die just like other living systems. As a living system, there are complex interdependencies that, in reality, govern the functionality of the organization and how it successfully responds to change. A growth culture embracing flexibility and order can incorporate at the same time the mindset of being and becoming despite the inherent conflict between the two. Therefore, we must understand the dynamics of the culture and how it interplays with actions of the organization in different circumstances.

It would be safe to say that organizations are established through human thought. This process starts with a lot of thinking and planning, which then can lead to the actual establishment of an organization, interchangeably termed a *company* in the context of this article. In other words, the emergent company is planned and conceived by an individual or individuals who are governed by their thoughts and ideas.

When established, the company grows, matures, and ages just like any other living system. In its infancy, the system is very flexible but unpredictable. As we know, young infants are very flexible, both physically and mentally; they are responding to needs as they arise. In other words, there are no *thoughts* that govern their actions, just needs. As infants age, thought enters more into the picture; over time, as they mature, they learn to synchronize actions and thoughts and there is a greater degree of order or predictability in play. As humans age, they lose the ability to synchronize thoughtful flexibility and order and become rigid and resistant to change. This process starts with their way of thinking, which blocks the natural way of perceiving a situation and reacting to it both timely and successfully. As living and thinking systems, companies are experiencing the same evolutionary forces because they are also governed by human thought.

Given that organizations are established and governed by thoughts, there are certain consequences that have a profound influence on organizational resiliency. Organizations are a composition of the collective thoughts of its members or employees. Given that thoughts run us and our organizations, it is interesting to consider some of the inherent flaws in the thinking process, which, in many ways can be considered the primary factors contributing to either resilience in change or destruction of the system.

Each of us has our own personal history and memory that influence the way we see the world and the expectations and hopes we have for it. This is significant in that the key to anticipating the future and preparing the organization for changes is our foresight, which is affected by our past experiences. Past beliefs, hopes, and commitments—in other words, past memories—influence our current behavior and how we perceive what is happening. Furthermore, current behavior is influenced by how we perceive the future. Keeping these fundamental features in mind, it follows that attitudes and values are resistant to change.

Attitudes and values resistant to change means that we tend to judge the future by the past, which manifests itself in statements like: "We have tried this before," "Things will brighten up as before," "Nothing to worry, this is not the first time," and so forth. This, along with thoughts leading us unconsciously away from the real situation—adapting to the situation by perceiving it differently—is one of the most profound death traps since it undermines resilience through the belief that: "Things are not really what they seem."

Another major factor undermining resilience is the human desire for equilibrium. We seek balance and security, which, when things are good, we hope can go on forever unchanged. Yet, according to the theory of thermodynamics, equilibrium is the end state in the evolution of closed systems and the point at which the system no longer has capacity for change. By seeking equilibrium, we are trying to transform the living human system into a closed system, whereas everything alive is an open system that engages with its environment and continues to grow. Again, we are inadvertently led to thinking that the development of the company toward stability and order is desirable when, in the long term, it leads to undesirable aging and decline.

During change, things fall apart and need to be integrated in a new way. We cannot continue doing things as before and need to find new ways, which often can feel disturbing and even painful. Everything points to increased rates of change and volatility and with more profound effects than ever before. Yet, we fail to realize that openness to the environment and constant struggle between disintegration and integration, over time, spawns a stronger and adaptive system, which is not as vulnerable to external pressures. Through adaptation skills and controlled flexibility, the organization as a human system develops increasing autonomy from the environment and develops new capacities that make it increasingly resourceful. That is what we call real resilience.

In traditional organizational development thinking, people believe that too much freedom will disturb the necessary order and stability and thus must be governed. In reality, resilience and the ability to be stable in a changing environment is gained by supporting change within the system itself. As a result, freedom and order, believed to work against each other, are actually partnering factors in generating resilience (see Figure 1).

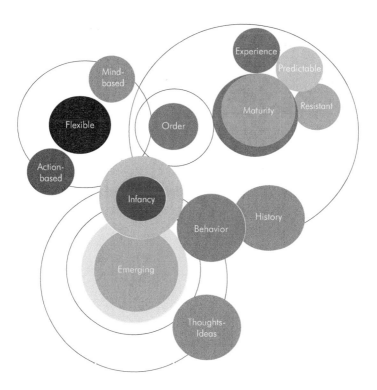

Figure 1. Agile and resilient organization as a living system.

As stated, organizations are living systems. Contrary to most other living systems, however, organizations can live forever if the interplay between flexibility and order are constantly nurtured and maintained. If not, organizations age like any other systems and eventually die. Thus, the real-life threatening factor in organizational life is that the natural human desire for order slowly kills the entrepreneurship within the organization, which causes it to age. If this happens, the aging culture of the organization causes it to unconsciously drift toward stability and create an ever-growing resistance to change, turning into denial and flawed perception of reality. Turning the desire for equilibrium into a positive force, on the other hand, comes with conscious efforts to bring about change or throw the organization off balance, regularly seeking a new balance, which in the process strengthens the organization and makes it more resilient. Once things have been stabilized, change is needed like a body that needs movement to stay agile.

At this point, it is appropriate to bring perseverance into the picture. Perseverance is defined by *Merriam-Webster Dictionary* as "the continued effort to do or achieve something despite difficulties, failure, or opposition." Perseverance and resilience go hand in hand when coping with the increasingly VUCA environment. While resilience is needed to recover quickly from crises, perseverance is the key ingredient for resilience.

## Flexibility and Order

We have pointed out that what makes organizations resilient is their constant efforts to embrace change through flexibility and reintegrating its elements through order and governance. We have also pointed out that within organizations, run by human thought, there is an inherent conflict between desire for flexibility and the need for control and order. The question is: Is there an optimal point for balance between flexibility and control?

We think it is important to distinguish between the flexibility of the mind, or perhaps rather culture, and the flexibility of the system as such. We can measure the flexibility of cultures, the readiness to make a change, idea generation, innovation, and other elements of the planning process as such. One thing to consider is *change* and *being ready* to make a change whenever necessary. Another thing is actually *making the change*. One flexibility is mind based and the other is action; these need to go hand in hand if the organization is to be resilient. Too often, there are actions without thought on one hand, which include high risks, even danger. On the other hand, there are thoughts without action, which is riskier and even more dangerous. Therefore, control needs to be implemented to govern the movements of the ever-growing organization or system and, with increasing maturity, the capacity to control both mind and movements becomes stronger.

Control can be defined in two ways. An administrative control, which manifests itself in explicit processes, routines, monitoring, and so forth; whereas mind-based control is more about tacit and unwritten laws, values, knowledge, routines, and so forth. We see the administrative control at its greatest in bureaucracies, which operate with the mindset, that "if anything happens here, we are ready!" Mind-based control is at its greatest in mature organizations where the unwritten laws and ways of thinking have followed unconscious routines (reflexes) for so long that they govern the ways people act and think.

This leads to the conclusion that if an organization is to be resilient, both flexibility and control are desirable, as stated earlier. Considering thought and action as two sides of the same coin, it is important to combine flexibility in thought and mind-based control. This is not for the purpose of suppressing entrepreneurship and innovation, but to use mind-based control play as the countering role to strengthen the decision-making process. This is when mind-based control is in the forms of strong shared mission and values that focus the organization's energy on the desired or required direction. This means that it matters what we decide to do and when and we cannot do whatever whenever. When making a movement or taking action, administrative control is desirable to control our movements so that we can move in a predictable and efficient manner in whatever we put our minds to. It is important to note that the combination of mind-based flexibility and control needs to be the *driving force*; the combination of action-based flexibility and control is the *driven force* to secure we don't lose the organic dynamics that keep the system alive and strong.

## Case in Point

Taking an example of a large power and utility company in Iceland, Reykjavik Energy built a strong governance of strategic implementation before the COVID-19 crisis.

The foundations of a strategic culture would, however, never have been so deep rooted if it had not been for the strong leadership of the CEO. The CEO, with support from the board of directors had, in the years leading up to the pandemic, placed emphasis on continuous improvements in strategic management. With a unique Ownership Strategy that the owners of the company (three municipalities) had formulated in 2012, the focus had been on applying the governance at hand to support the Strategy Execution Management. The process that had been put in place—strategic corporate governance—ensured that despite the challenges, the organizations did not throw away the owners' vision of creating a better future for society in a sustainable manner.

The process included continuous revisions of strategy, policies, objects, and goals and entailed assigning a responsible party for each policy that ensures its revision and follow-up on goals. The responsible party had to abide by a yearly revision plan, which entailed presenting the revised strategy and goals while being accountable for the outcome. As a token of the strong strategic management focus, the organization was among the first in Iceland to hire a corporate strategic officer to implement and oversee the process of strategic corporate governance. With this focus on corporate strategic management, the organization was able to respond quickly to changes in the external as well as the internal environments and adapt their execution plan toward their vision. This made the organization adaptable and flexible—with some degree of order—to respond to change and challenges, being resilient, and adjusting easily to change.

## Conclusion

In this article we started by outlining that a crisis has two faces: one involving a threat and the other an opportunity. We also pointed out that the more severe the crisis, the larger potential for opportunities, which points to the fact that some of history's greatest human innovations and achievements were conceived during crises.

We have covered the insights leaders need to cultivate in an ever-changing environment. We have emphasized the fact that organizations are created and run by human thoughts; thus, the way of thinking is a determinant factor for their functionality and ability to adapt. Organizations are comprised of humans and, as such, organizations can be viewed as organic living systems or rather, human systems. These are constantly on the move consciously or unconsciously, with complex interdependencies among elements of the organization, whether it be humans or the processes developed through human thought. Therefore, we need to consider the organization as a holistic system, meaning that we need to adapt it as a whole, not just parts of it.

When thinking about organizations as living systems going through life cycle stages, we also need to consider that the challenge is to avoid stagnancy through the embedded human quest for an equilibrium. This requires constantly challenging the system and throwing it off balance to harness the human need to seek new balance and, in the process, creating an ever stronger and more resilient organization. In doing so, the interplay between mind and actions needs to be kept in mind at all times.

To thrive in an increasingly volatile, uncertain, complex, and ambiguous (VUCA) operational environment, leaders must have *bringing about a cultural evolution* on their agendas. This evolution needs to lead to a growth mindset, fostering entrepreneurship and innovation by challenging equilibrium that brings about stagnation, resulting in a loss of capacity for change. The core elements of being able to apply flexibility and order in a constructive way is to operate with mind-based flexibility and order as the driving force and action flexibility and order as the driven force. This requires time and attention to carefully establish a shared vision and goals at all levels, which will drive engagement of all members of the organization. Embedding the needed way of thinking and doing into the cultural DNA of the organization will improve its immunity to change through resilience. Thus, if resilience is defined as the ability to recover or adjust easily to change, the objective of organizations must be to constantly adapt through resilience.

We illustrated the case of an Icelandic group of companies having enforced a strategic process of order, or control, and constantly challenging death by equilibrium with encouraging flexibility. This leadership meant carefully crafting and following through a cultural evolution by embracing challenges, enabling the organization to become agile, and responding to opportunities and seizing them. This gave the group the advantage of fostering innovation by throwing the system off balance, strengthening it, and making it more resilient through a strategic process as part of their governance.

## About the Authors

**Gudrun Erla Jonsdottir** is the Chief Strategy Officer at Reykjavik Energy, the largest power and utility company in Iceland. As a strategy officer, she is responsible for sustaining and communicating the future vision and execution of the corporate strategy. Her role includes being both a creative thinker and an influential collaborator. She is a visionary, ensuring that execution supports the strategy elements.

Prior to her position at Reykjavik Energy, she was the Managing Director for Husavik Energy. She served as Director for Samorka, the Federation of Energy and Utility Companies in Iceland from 2012 and was Vice Chairman from 2016 until 2019, and has been Chairman of Veitur Utilities since 2018. She is a PhD candidate at the University of Iceland and holds an MSc degree in Marketing and International Business Administration. Her PhD research on Ownership Strategy, a novel strategic governance tool, has ignited the interest of both academics and practitioners, internationally and abroad, showing that her research is highly relevant and practical.

**Bjarni Snæbjörn Jónsson** is a cofounder and CSO at DecideAct A/S, a Danish software company offering SaaS digital solutions for effective execution of strategies and change.

Bjarni has a Cand.oecon degree from the University of Iceland, an MBA from the University of Michigan Ross School of Business, and a PhD in Organizational Transformation from the Adizes Graduate School in California. Since 1995, Bjarni has consulted with organizations throughout the private and public sectors, assisting in the management of organizational change and development. His academic interests, apart from strategy execution management, are primarily on large-scale human system change and evolution.

# Building Organizational Resilience: When the Entire Organization Should Be Engaged and Power Unleashed

THOMAS KEIL AND MARIANNA ZANGRILLO

10

The series of shocks over the past five years has strongly underlined the importance of organizational resilience, which is an organization's ability "to anticipate, prepare for, respond and adapt to incremental change and sudden disruptions to survive and prosper" (Denyer, 2017). Shocks, such as the COVID-19 pandemic and the Ukraine war, have challenged the operating assumptions of organizations and forced changes along almost all dimensions of the business, often over brief periods of time. How can leadership teams effectively deal with such changes?

Many organizations have looked again at the traditional strong leader approach, where a powerful individual almost single-handedly makes decisions and drives the organization through unexpected high waves like a skipper of a sailboat through a storm. The idea underlying this response is that by centralizing decision-making, the organization can better muster a coordinated and effective response to the change. For instance, following the COVID-19 outbreak, much discussion initially revolved around the idea that centralized leadership, such as that in China under Xi Jinping, may be better able to take decisive action in response to challenges arising from the spread of the novel virus. Similarly, SAP (a large German software company) announced the discontinuation of a co-CEO arrangement to streamline decision-making in response to the COVID-19 crisis in the business domain.

This article argues that decision centralization and hiring leaders who prefer to make and drive decisions by themselves may only be a fix for the short run that allows a quick response. In many instances, it is a counterproductive strategy in the long run and may run counter to building systematic organizational resilience. Instead, we argue that organizations need to develop resilience as a core competence of their top teams with individuals who can complement one another and have different styles and capabilities to address various challenges as they emerge. Additionally, the importance of building the foundations of resilience across different layers of the organization should not be neglected. We propose some simple principles to help achieve this.

## The Challenge of Organizational Shocks

Organizations and their management teams are creatures of habit. To achieve stability and replicate success, organizations routinize how they run their businesses, encapsulating a recipe for what works and what does not. If successful, these recipes and the assumptions they are built on will be questioned less and less, and the starting point or the context within which those assumptions were generated may be forgotten. Furthermore, management teams are likely not to question such success recipes, even more so when the experience within the team is relatively homogeneous. After all, if everyone has the same experience handling things, who should suggest a different approach?

Environmental changes and any disruptive shock fundamentally threaten these routines and their underlying assumptions. The COVID-19 pandemic raised fundamental questions on well-functioning routines regarding market forecasts or global supply chains, not to mention broader topics such as how people work and make decisions. Existing solutions stopped working from one day to the next; management teams were faced with the situation of needing to rethink about how to do business when demand from one day to the next disappeared; supplies from factories around the globe became unavailable; employees no longer could come to the office; and management teams no longer could meet in person to make decisions around informal dinners or other events. Similarly, the Russian invasion of Ukraine has fundamentally challenged firms to rethink where they will do business and how they will respond to a changing political climate.

In this situation, existing solutions stop working. Still, alternatives are not immediately available, and simple things, such as managing a crisis, which most companies are ready to do on paper, become a hurdle almost impossible to surpass. Management teams need to devise a swift response to the shock and manage its impact on the business in the short term. But, in the cases of the COVID-19 pandemic and the Russian invasion of Ukraine, they also need to revisit the very assumptions about the business going forward to reconstruct new routines, which will make the business sustainable in the long term.

Organizations capable of mustering effective responses in both the short term and the long term are clearly at an advantage during such periods of change. In other words, change and crisis will destroy organizations that do not have a DNA fit for survival and drive the selection of the new winners.

## The Lure of Decision Centralization

A common strategy to deal with shocks has been decision centralization because that allows more speed and firm actions. In light of a disruptive shock, it has become more obvious that standard responses are no longer effective. Airlines faced with a reduction of 85% of their revenues, as occurred during the COVID-19 pandemic, or manufacturing firms faced with the complete stop of production of key suppliers—as occurred both during the COVID-19 pandemic and the Russian invasion of Ukraine—can simply no longer respond as in the past. However, the correct response is rarely apparent, and different leaders in the organization may hold different views on what to do. Therefore, a strong leader at the top may appear to be a mechanism to break through the stalemate among different opinions and positions and arrive at a decision.

A strong leader at the center may also provide a simple and coherent vision of the response—no matter how right or wrong that vision may be—compared to the cacophony of voices that a decentralized decision-making process may produce under high uncertainty. One just needs to compare the simple message (e.g., zero COVID-19 cases) that China's Xi Jinping provided in centralized China in response to COVID-19 with the myriad voices in the decentralized West. And last, but not least, should the leader be proven wrong, a scapegoat for the failure is readily at hand for everyone else since it wasn't their own decision after all.

## Why Decision Centralization Rarely Works in the Long Run

In light of a disruptive shock, centralization may solve the problem of quickly arriving at a decision that can be implemented fast. And if the leader at the center of the organization gets the response right, it might be very effective in the short run, as virtually no other approach will deliver a decision with the same speed.

The problem with centralization is that it does not create a systematic organizational capability for resilience. Instead, it creates the exact opposite: an organization dependent on an individual savior. And just as problematic, if that savior proves to be less capable and makes the wrong call, if the organization keeps relying on their judgment with later changes (and an individual alone cannot always get it right), or the leader turns into a tyrant, the organization may find itself in a worsening situation over time. As we now see with Vladimir Putin in Russia, many other autocratic leaders in history, and many organizations built solely around one CEO's decision-making, the results can be catastrophic.

Centralizing decision-making tends to weed out new and diverging information, even more with larger organizations, since the leader at the center is simply too far away from the real challenges or may not hear about them early enough. Centralization puts trust in the leader's capability where solid discussion of options should occur. Finally, over time, centralization can weed out initiative throughout the organization both in terms of proposing options and implementing decisions, as members outside the leader's inner circle become disengaged and talent starts to leave the organization.

## Building Organizational Resilience

For the organization to consistently respond to changes and disruptions over time, resilience needs to be organizational and not dependent on a single individual at the center. These simple principles may help anchor resilience in the organization rather than the individual:

**Build your management team to focus simultaneously on the short term and the long run.** Organizations are often laser focused on building effective management teams for the here and now. However, to build organizational resilience, the focus on the short term may not address future challenges. A focus on what leaders could need in the long run should be in place to have a sustainable pipeline with recurring and diverse leadership options, which can address different situations and ultimately prepare the organization for possible future shocks. Moreover, management teams need to develop the ability to not lose focus on the long-term trends even when short-term pressures loom large. For instance, a sequence of shocks, such as the COVID-19 pandemic followed by the Ukraine war, can easily lead to focus on dealing with the current shocks, while taking eyes off long-run trends such as industry changes, digitalization, and sustainability. Instead, it would be more reasonable to view the shocks as an opportunity to accelerate progress and prepare the organization for changes that otherwise could be difficult to implement. For instance, the responses needed to deal with the COVID-19 pandemic have allowed some organizations to progress on digitalization at a pace hitherto completely unimaginable. "Never leave a good crisis go to waste," as Winston Churchill said, when he was working to form the United Nations after World War II to create international resilience to future political crises.

**Be decisive but don't forget to generate and weigh the options.**
Resilience, particularly in light of a dramatic shock, means acting with both speed and quality when the need arises. Either one alone is a recipe for failure. A fast response without sufficient consideration of the available options may lead to poor decisions that may worsen the situation. Lengthy weighing of options may lead to finding the seemingly best solutions but may be too late to be effective. To balance speed and quality, a diverse management team can prove to be a real asset as it may allow generating the needed breadth of options, arguments, and opinions fast enough. In particular, under the time pressure and high stakes of a crisis, decision-making process matters and should not be left to chance. Instead, decision-making processes in a time of crisis can be improved through regular training, as the example of organizations focusing on crisis response show.

**Respond as a group and don't allow profiteering.** A central principle to making resilience organizational is to curb the profiteering of individual leaders during a crisis. Entrepreneurial individuals often try to use crises to their advantage at the organization's cost. While individual initiative and entrepreneurial behavior are essential to identify opportunities and responses to change, particularly in crises, they need to be balanced against the coordination required to avoid individuals who may take the opportunity to optimize their personal or unit's benefit without considering the broader picture. The attempt of Shell's oil traders to gain from sanctions against Russian oil firms at the beginning of the Russian invasion may serve as an example of such profiteering at the expense of the organization's interests. Although the traders managed to realize a short-term financial benefit, the resulting public outcry against Shell created a massive loss in public trust and ultimately forced Shell to forgo the benefits from the trade. Instead, crises should emphasize behavior of mutual support, such that the individual members of the leadership team go forward or stand back and bend as needed to make the organization go forward and emerge stronger. Individually taken, each leader should be able to fall and get up stronger with the lending hand of another member who can stand at the same time.

**Lead from the center, but engage all layers of the organization.** To build resilience in the long run, organizations need to systematically engage all layers of the organization, because no part can operate in a vacuum and various aspects and knowledge must be utilized to resolve diverse matters, ensuring that the customer and operations are always considered. As important as top management is in leading the organization in a crisis, leaders need to encourage the development of future-proof solutions throughout the organization and bring them systematically to the core to leverage the intelligence of the whole organization rather than relying on the sights and ideas of a few. For instance, organizations such as Nestlé, which successfully responded during the COVID-19 pandemic, focused on setting frameworks from the top within which solutions could emerge from all layers of the organization.

## Conclusion

In today's turbulent times, leadership quality is more important than ever, with more leaders than just the top team needing to play important roles. Organizations must meet higher expectations than ever, at a speed that was simply unimaginable until a few years ago; this can only happen when a diverse enough set of individuals can contribute and the right ones can jump in to help, depending on what sudden new challenge appears. To make resilience a reliable organizational capability, it is necessary that strong leaders step back somewhat and leave room for the entire organization to grow. Thus, the organization-wide foundation will become more solid and reliable, far beyond the individual.

## Reference

Denyer, D. (2017). *Organizational resilience: A summary of academic evidence, business insights and new thinking*. British Standards Institution and Cranfield School of Management.

## About the Authors

**Thomas Keil** and **Marianna Zangrillo** are internationally recognized authorities on CEO, leadership, and strategy topics and coauthors of *The Next CEO: Board and CEO Perspectives for Successful CEO Succession* (Routledge, 2021) and *The Next Leadership Team: How to Select, Build, and Optimize Your Top Leadership Team* (Routledge, 2023).

# Resilient Leadership: How to Build Resilience and Help Your Team Thrive

SUSIE KENNEDY

**11**

The final paragraph of George S. Everly's *Harvard Business Review* article of 24 June 2011 is thought provoking (Everly, 2011). Everly's suggestion that in 2011 "To say we live in challenging times is an understatement" leaves us, by comparison in 2022, with few adjectives to describe these times, other than *these times*. Just as the world is learning to cope with the COVID-19 global pandemic of the last two years, grapple with economic recovery, face the impact of climate change, and ongoing political and social challenges, on 24 February 2022 Russia invaded Ukraine, posing a massive geopolitical threat. At the time of this writing, the war is still raging and the outlook is precarious. On 14 April 2022, Reuters News reported: "Russia warns of nuclear, hypersonic deployment if Sweden and Finland join NATO." (Reuters, 2022)

The impact of the war thus far has been profound and far reaching. According to Jacob Kern of the World Food Programme (WFP), more than 10 million people in Ukraine have been displaced in one month alone, a level that took 10 years to reach in Syria (Saladino, 2022). Oil prices, already inflated, have soared, significantly increasing the cost of living (Kolaczkowski, 2022). Grain, vegetable oil, and fertilizer prices have all increased due to supply shortages from Ukraine and Russia, leading to inflated food prices, the threat of poverty, and perils of protectionism.

Many governments are imposing sanctions on Russia and its oligarchs, restricting trade and travel, and seizing assets. Nearly 600 companies have curtailed operations in Russia (Yale School of Management, 2022), many voluntarily, others prompted by media criticism. Even the United Kingdom's Chancellor of the Exchequer faced questions about connections to Russia through his wife's family business, Infosys, which at the time still had an office in Moscow (*Economic Times*, 2022).

Looking forward, threats of the rise of far-right nationalism, the return of former U.S. President Donald J. Trump in 2024, and the global divide in support for Russia (*Economist*, 2022), suggest continued geopolitical and economic instability. Arguably, the only thing we can be certain about is that uncertainty and disruption will continue to dominate.

These times require **resilient leadership**, meaning the ability to develop one's own resilience, prepare for future crises, and help teams thrive in challenging conditions. This article will consider how leaders can build resilience by including our research conducted during the COVID-19 crisis and lessons from leading in an uncertain natural environment.

## First Develop Your Own Resilience

We are reminded by Peter F. Drucker that, "a person can perform only from strength." (Drucker, 2008) In these times, leaders must strengthen their ability to cope with crises in order to help their team thrive. Making time for reflection is one way to identify resilience strength.

In *Upheaval: How Nations Cope with Crisis and Change*, Jared Diamond describes 12 factors, which, according to crisis therapists, make it more or less likely that a person will succeed in coping with a crisis (Table 1, Diamond, 2020). He goes on to draw comparisons between how individuals and nations cope with crises. These factors are relevant to resilient leaders too. For example, Diamond suggests that in relation to the factor, *experience of previous personal crisis*, "If you have already had the experience of coping successfully with some different crisis in the past, that gives you more confidence that you can solve the new crisis as well."

**Table 1.** *Related to the Outcomes of Personal Crises* (Diamond, 2019)

Source: Diamond, G. M. (2019). *Upheaval: How nations cope with crisis and change* (Table 1.1, p. 39) Penguin.

1. Acknowledgment that one is in crisis.
2. Acceptance of one's personal responsibility to do something.
3. Building a fence to delineate one's individual problems needing to be solved.
4. Getting material and emotional help from other individuals and groups.
5. Using other individuals as role models of how to solve problems.
6. Ego strength.
7. Honest self-appraisal.
8. Experience of previous personal crises.
9. Patience.
10. Flexible personality.
11. Individual core values.
12. Freedom from personal constraints.

We have been researching this area to find out how senior managers in UK local government coped with the COVID-19 crisis since the start of the first lockdown in March 2020. We spoke with senior managers from 60 local authorities who were leading the COVID-19 response in various roles, including

**Table 2.** *Lessons From the COVID-19 Crisis* (KBA Solutions, 2022)

Source: KBA Solutions Limited (April 2022). *Lessons from Covid crisis that will help in the future.* Research in UK local government. Responses from senior management in 60 local authorities March 2020–March 2022.

1. Individuals and organizations experience crisis in different ways.
2. You and your organization are more resilient than you thought.
3. Leaders must be compassionate and adapt their style to understand the needs of each individual.
4. Communicate frequently using different methods and focus on well-being.
5. Teams can work better together and collaborate more.
6. Crisis creates the opportunity to innovate.
7. New systems and ways of working are more efficient.
8. Look after yourself.

responsibility for freeing up ICU beds by moving patients into nursing homes, establishing temporary mortuary sites, and distributing emergency food parcels to vulnerable residents.

We asked them to reflect on the question: *"What have you learned about yourself and your organization that can help you in the future?"* Analysis of the responses concluded eight key lessons, which were surprisingly positive and optimistic given the scale of challenges this sector has faced (Table 2).

A significant outcome of the research was that the act of reflection boosted managers' confidence because it helped them realize how successful they were in coping with the crisis. We have incorporated these lessons in our suggestions for building resilient leadership in these three key areas:

- Look after yourself
- Prepare for the next crisis
- Help your team thrive

## Look After Yourself

This sounds obvious, but it can be difficult to maintain well-being, especially when juggling homeschooling, childcare, and other responsibilities while under pressure to deliver results. Yet it is essential to stay fit and healthy to build resilience. Practical suggestions to help boost personal resilience include:

1. Get enough sleep, eat well, and exercise regularly. Our research showed during the COVID-19 crisis many managers experienced frustration, stress, and anxiety. Getting enough sleep, ideally 7 to 8 hours, yields major well-being benefits and can combat these effects (Walker, 2017). Sleep helps improve our decision-making, including the decisions about what we eat and how we exercise. So prioritizing sleep is essential for building resilience.
2. Reflect on what you have learned about yourself. The discipline of taking time for reflection, ideally with colleagues or a coach, pays off. As shown above, managers' confidence was boosted by realizing how resilient they were. They recognized the crisis gave them the opportunity to seek improvements, and that new systems and new ways of working were more efficient than during prepandemic times. These insights provided new energy for tackling the next challenge.
3. Build a network of relationships to gain the support you need. We gain different types of support from different relationships. For example, colleagues can provide practical support by sharing workload and resources. Your boss can give you confidence by supporting you. Your friends can provide emotional support by listening to your frustrations; so, investing in relationships helps build resilience. Interestingly, our research indicated the combined effect of working from home in a less formal environment and increased frequency of online meetings—with more time devoted to well-being/social issues—appeared to increase trust and make it easier to build supportive relationships within teams and with stakeholders.
4. Take control and give it up. As mentioned above, managers can experience stress, anxiety, and feel overwhelmed with their workload. With support, it is possible to take more control over your workload and create well-being time for yourself. Building a support network can help, as can simple acts such as changing technology settings to stop events from being automatically added to your calendar. Honing your digital skills to stay technically savvy will help you feel more confident. But you may also need to give up control. Be honest with yourself about how flexible you are and whether you are risking burnout because you won't let go. Are you delegating enough? Do you think only you can deliver

the right outcome? Must you chair every team meeting? Giving up some control can decrease your stress and give others new opportunities, so it's worthwhile getting some honest feedback about areas where you can give up control.

## Prepare for the Next Crisis

Professional backcountry ski guide and author, Rob Coppolillo works in a permanently uncertain, often dangerous natural environment guiding ski touring recreationists in North America and Europe. In his book, *The Ski Guide Manual*, recommended by the American Mountain Guides Association, we can learn many lessons to develop resilience by being prepared. For Coppolillio, planning and preparation are crucial: "Our trip plan offers solutions and mitigation strategies before we find ourselves exposed to hazards like avalanches, rock and ice falls, dangerous cold or hot weather, or the disconnect of an incompatible team." (Coppolillo, 2020, p. 2) His approach to planning, based on the American Institute for Avalanche Research and Education (AIARE) Risk Management Framework includes these activities:

- Stay fit and healthy.
- Track the season's conditions.
- Practice rescue.
- Learn about avalanches.
- Become an expert navigator.
- Investigate route options.
- Find compatible partners.
- Get your gear ready.

Planning and preparation start late summer/early fall so that "when the backcountry finally fills in, you want to be ready mentally and physically." (Coppolillo, 2020, p. 3)

In the same way professional ski guides prepare to stay mentally and physcially fit, have the right equipment, build knowledge of the environment and expertise to cope with it, plan their routes, and manage the team, so too must resilient leaders. Activities that help prepare for future uncertainty and build resilience can be distilled into the following key areas:

1. Clarify purpose. A recent Deloitte report indicates the importance of purpose orientation in building organizational resilience (Deloitte, 2021). On a personal level, individuals with a strong sense of purpose tend to be motivated, with a passion for learning, developing, growing, and performing. A strong sense of purpose builds personal resilience, which in turn can cultivate a more engaged and resilient team and organization. This is consistent with our research, which found teams worked better because they shared a strong common purpose and values during the crisis. Leaders should routinely remind themselves of their own purpose and help their teams do the same so that everyone is mentally ready for the next challenge.

2. Know what's coming up. Ski guides track conditions so they can assess the implications on avalanche risk later in the season. Pressure to deliver results can make it challenging for leaders to maintain strategic focus—to be able to see the wood for the trees. Yet, leaders need to be aware of the issues they are likely to face and plan for them. Using tools, such as PESTLE (an analysis that studies the key external factors affecting an organization, such as political, economic, sociological, technological, legal, and environmental factors), Scenario Analysis, and MoSCoW (must-have, should-have, could-have, won't-have), leaders can engage stakeholders in regular joint decision-making and problem-solving activities, capturing the advantages of divergent thinking styles. This approach is likely to result in better quality decisions and closer relationships.

3. Build a flexible, adaptable workforce. The events of 2020 highlighted the importance of a flexible and adaptable workforce in building resilience. The Deloitte survey found three in four respondents who had taken steps to build flexibility had a more resilient culture. Leaders can build resilience in their workforce by having processes that facilitate easy redeployment (and meet ethical and legal standards), by recruiting staff for a learning mindset rather than a specific skill set, and by training staff in new skills including curiosity, creativity, and empathy (Renjen, 2021).

4. Resilience reviews. Deloitte suggests organizations have been forced to think more holistically about resilience within interlinked pillars. In preparing for future crises, leaders can review their financial resilience to ensure they can withstand impacts on income, assets, and liquidity. A review of operational resilience to ensure business continuity will include reviewing investment in technology. A review of reputational resilience will ensure the goodwill and trust of stakeholders necessary to cope in challenging times (Renjen, 2021).

**Table 3.** *Diagnostic Tool—Conditions for a Thriving High-Performing Team* (KBA Solutions, 2018)

Source: KBA Solutions Limited (2018). These factors form the basis of our diagnostic tool to help leaders and teams develop high performance.

---

1. The team knows its purpose and common goal are compelling and motivating.

2. The team has meaningful and effective performance objectives.

3. The team has freedom to choose how it completes projects/tasks and accountability for delivery.

4. The team feels senior leadership expects it will achieve high standards and supports them (Pygmalion Effect).

5. The team has complimentary skills, including interpersonal, problem-solving, technical, and learning skills.

6. The team has agreed on ways of working and meaningful norms of behavior.

7. Individual team members believe their role in the team meets their personal development and social needs (feel valued, shown respect, and treated fairly).

8. Team members get to know each other and build relationships so they feel comfortable giving feedback about the team and tasks.

9. There is a shared belief that team members will not be punished or humiliated for speaking up with ideas, questions, concerns, or mistakes (psychological safety).

10. Excellent performance is celebrated and rewarded.

---

A final note is to remind leaders to be wary of devoting time unequally to more favorable preparatory activities. Coppilollo says: "The irony is, we often spend more time researching and buying a new set of skis than we do refining our skills for the upcoming winter." (Coppolillo, 2020, p.3)

## Help Your Team Thrive

In the mountains, Coppilollo chooses to ski with high-performing teams as, he argues: "High-performing teams keep us safer, find better skiing, and have more fun too." (Coppolillo, 2020, p. 165) They reduce uncertainty by checking assumptions and collaborative decision-making. The role of the resilient leader is to create the conditions that allow their team to thrive and be high performing.

Over the last two years we have researched managers' responses to the question: "What conditions allow your people to thrive?" Analysis of responses indicated seven categories of conditions:

1. Psychological safety
2. Physical safety, health, well-being, and work environment
3. Clear purpose and vision
4. Autonomy and empowerment
5. Challenge and achievement
6. Skills and learning opportunity
7. Teamwork

We noted psychological safety was, by far, the most frequently cited condition for thriving. We also noted conditions for thriving as identified by managers in the survey mapped to our conditions for a thriving high-performing team (Table 3). This indicates the managers know what conditions they need to create to help their people and teams to thrive.

However, while managers know *what* conditions they need to create, *how* to go about creating them can be more or less challenging. For example, creating a shared purpose, common goal, performance objectives, and ways of working is relatively straightforward to achieve, whereas psychological safety is more complicated. Amy Edmondson, Novartis Professor of Leadership at Harvard Business School, introduced this factor. In *The Fearless Organization* she says, "Psychological safety is broadly defined as a climate in which people are comfortable expressing themselves," and explains, "They are confident they can speak up and won't be humiliated, ignored or blamed." (Edmondson, 2019, p. xvi)

It is particularly important in uncertain, high-consequence environments, as Coppolillo recognizes, "We need to continuously create and foster a sense of psychological safety among teammates." He argues it is a continuous priority, "not something we do in the fall and then let it grow stale throughout the winter. It requires ongoing attention, in guide meetings and trip plans with buddies." (Coppopillo, 2020, p. 157)

A few practical ways resilient leaders can create the conditions for a high-performing team include:

1. Diagnose and prescribe. The leader can carry out an assessment of the extent to which the conditions exist that allow the team to be high performing using a diagnostic tool such as the KBA tool listed in Table 3. Team members then individually complete the diagnostic with the support of a coach who can then analyze all of the responses and present the findings, initially to the leader and then in a group coaching

workshop with everyone together. The team can then prescribe its own team development plan to create the conditions for high performance. Having created the plan themselves, they are more likely to follow it.

2. Learn how to create psychological safety. Creating psychological safety is difficult because it is contingent on the leader creating a positive climate. It means learning a set of new behaviors and skills in order to create shared expectations, the atmosphere, and structures to give people confidence to speak up and to enable continous learning. Resilient leaders create a positive, supportive environment by demonstrating behaviors, such as consulting team members, asking them for input, showing concern for team members as individuals, and by using positive language/body language.

Creating and maintaining a positive, supportive environment can be difficult to maintain when under pressure. Sometimes espoused behaviors are inconsistent with behaviors demonstrated, such as in the case of the manager who routinely reminds her team she has an open door policy but fails to be supportive when the team makes a mistake. Amy Edmondson has developed a comprehensive toolkit for developing psychological safety and recommends leaders routinely take a leadership self-reflection assessment to help their development (Edmondson, 2019).

## So What?

Resilience is a strength leaders can develop. The resilient leader is mindful of the factors that help them succeed in coping with a crisis. They look after themselves physically and mentally. They prepare for the next crisis by ensuring maximum flexibility and adaptability and they create the conditions that allow their teams to become high performing.

As a human race, we are still here because we continue to develop resilience and help others to thrive. That is the essence of resilient leadership.

## References

Coppolillo, R., & Zacharias, C. (2020). *The ski guide manual: Advanced techniques for the backcountry* (Manuals Series) (1st ed.). Falcon Guides.
Deloitte. (2021). *The resilient organization. How to thrive in the face of uncertainty.* https://www2.deloitte.com/ca/en/pages/risk/articles/the-resilient-organization.html?icid=learn_more_content_click
Diamond, J. (2020). *Upheaval: How nations cope with crisis and change.* Penguin.

Drucker, P. (2008). *Managing oneself*. Harvard Business Review Classics. Harvard Business Review Press.

Economic Times. (2022). *UK finance minister Rishi Sunak questioned over Infosys presence in Moscow*. March 25. https://economictimes.indiatimes.com/news/international/world-news/uk-finance-minister-rishi-sunak-questioned-over-infosys-presence-in-moscow/articleshow/90432868.cms

Economist. (2022). *Who are Russia's supporters?* April 4. https://www.economist.com/graphic-detail/2022/04/04/who-are-russias-supporters.

Edmondson, A. (2019). *The fearless organization: Creating psychological safety in the workplace for learning, innovation, and growth*. John Wiley & Sons.

Everly, G. S. (2011). Building a resilient organizational culture. *Harvard Business Review*. June 24.

Kolaczkowski, M. (2022). *How does the war in Ukraine affect oil prices?* World Economic Forum. 4 March.

Renjen, P. (2021). *Building the resilient organization*. 2021 Deloitte Global Resilience Report. https://www2.deloitte.com/global/en/insights/topics/strategy/characteristics-resilient-organizations.html

Reuters. (2022). *Russia warns of nuclear, hypersonic deployment if Sweden and Finland join NATO*. Reuters. April 14.

Saladino, D. (2022). *The food programme: Ukraine the food dimension Part 2*. April 10. [Radio Broadcast] https://www.bbc.co.uk/sounds/play/m0016818

Walker, M. (2017). Top tips to get a better night's sleep and improve your health. *New Scientist*. October 11. https://www.newscientist.com/article/2149792-top-tips-to-get-a-better-nights-sleep-and-improve-your-health/#ixzz7QpEHxWBk

Yale School of Management. (2022). Over 600 companies have curtailed operations in Russia—But some remain. April 15. https://som.yale.edu/story/2022/over-600-companies-have-curtailed-operations-russia-some-remain

## About the Author

**Susie Kennedy** is senior partner of KBA Solutions Limited, which she founded in 1993. KBA specializes in executive development and change leadership consulting. Susie has contributed to a number of Thinkers50 publications; she is Programme Director for KBA's Institute of Leadership and Management Strategic Leadership program for senior managers, with programs in the University of Cambridge, Premier Foods, and nationally for UK Local Government at King's College London.

# Using the **IDEAS** Process to Build a Framework for Resilience

KAIHAN KRIPPENDORFF AND
CORI DOMBROSKI

12

On an average day in 1998, a technology-enabled, business-minded consumer likely would have been familiar with the company names Amazon, Apple, and Netflix. After a day at work, they might have come home to log into their Apple iMac desktop computer, browse best-selling books online at Amazon.com, and check their mailbox for the recent delivery of Netflix DVD rentals.

Today, in 2022, that consumer can hold the power of an iMac (plus much more) in the palm of their hand. They can purchase groceries from an Amazon Fresh store or order just about anything from Amazon's website to be dropped off at their door. And there's no need to check the mailbox—a full Netflix streaming catalog is available on their TV at the press of a button.

For these three companies, today's business models and offerings look vastly different than what was offered 20 years ago. A common trait of resilient companies is that they adapt and transform, not once but over and over again—as Amazon progressed from an online bookstore to a multifaceted online retailer, a marketplace, a pharmacy, and now a grocery store.

The resilient company consistently generates a spread of strategic options it can select from and return to continuously. Its strategy is not a static document, but a continually evolving set of strategic options that are born out of fluid conversations, shaped by a shared language across the organization. The language used to create strategy enhances the options people see and choose. It determines the behaviors that can foster a culture of innovation, agility, and constant transformation. It is alive and real, without conclusion, and enables an organization to consciously create its own dynamic future.

### The IDEAS Process

For the last 15 years at Outthinker, we have been using a five-step process to help hundreds of companies come up with portfolios of creative and disruptive strategic options. We've discovered that this process also offers a framework for managing an organization with resilience. Using this process, you'll come away with business model ideas to implement in the short term and a repeatable exercise for generating new solutions when disruption inevitably arises. The five steps spell out an easy-to-remember acronym: IDEAS (Imagine, Dissect, Expand, Analyze, Sell); and following them results in a living strategy that can iterate and flex when the unexpected occurs. The five steps are described as follows:

## 1. Imagine

To survive in a world that is constantly changing, you will need to continuously imagine and reimagine your ideal future. By practicing an exercise in strategic foresight, you can come up with a few plausible options for what your future state will look like in 10 years. John Hagel, an author, consultant, speaker, and entrepreneur with 40 years of success in Silicon Valley, recommends a practice called 'zoom out, zoom in.' Zoom out to visualize your 10- to 20-year horizon. What is your mission? What will your market environment look like? What big opportunities and trends could you target and address? Resist the temptation to stay confined to your current products or industry (imagine the limitations if Amazon had only looked ahead in the realm of online bookstores). Futurists, such as Faith Popcorn, warn that the biggest mistake most people make is trying to predict what's going to happen in the future based on what is currently happening and what has happened in the past. As we saw in our earlier examples—Amazon, Apple, and Netflix—the future 20 years out will most assuredly look drastically different than it does today. Peer to the fringes of your market and customer base. What trends do you see gaining traction on the edges? What do you imagine your competitors doing in 10 to 20 years?

Then, zoom in to the next six to 12 months. What are the two or three immediate initiatives you could pursue to move you closer to your ideal long-term state? What would have the biggest impact in accelerating your progression? What key metrics will you track to determine if you're making progress toward that long-term time horizon?

When disruption happens, your short-term imagined future will suddenly change. Many companies make the mistake of directing their attention to the disruption playing out in the present, right in front of them. But, if you've developed a clear view of your future goal, your long-term vision is likely to remain the same. You can adjust your near-term tactics and stay focused on your ideal future horizon.

## 2. Dissect

With your future vision firmly in mind, the next step is to break down your strategic challenge into component parts. We suggest outlining a *system map* to show causes and effects, including variables and their dependencies, so you can understand how changes in one variable affect others. There are two reasons for doing this:

- You may find a new leverage point—a new variable that you had not considered before and that your competition is not paying attention to. This can open the potential for you to do things that no one is expecting. Indeed, as Richard Rumelt argues, many breakthrough strategies stem from a company or leadership team finding a leverage point (or "crux" as Rumelt puts it) of a problem that others are overlooking. Tesla Motors sought to solve the sustainable energy problem by attacking demand rather than supply, for example.
- You may narrow the scope of the problem. You may find that parts of the problem are already solved and that you can get the best yield on your time, effort, and creativity by focusing on just a few issues.

Take a look at your short-term and long-term challenges from step one, and dissect them into component parts. What would need to be true in the short-term to move you toward your long-term ideal? This should help you come up with two to three drivers that, if successfully solved, will get you to your future vision. Use those drivers to plot a map that includes your long-term strategic mission, your primary drivers, and the short-term problems you will solve right now.

## 3. Expand

French philosopher Émile Chartier famously stated: "There's nothing more dangerous than an idea if it's the only one you have." In a recent interview, management expert Gary Hamel repeated that sentiment, explaining that your chance of landing on a truly game-changing strategy is arithmetically determined by the number of potential strategic options you create in the first place. In short, the more options you and your team have in front of you, the more likely you will find the silver bullet.

Historically, it has been possible for a company to focus on one or just a few areas of their business model and achieve a lasting competitive advantage. BMW was known for having high quality and a wide range of products. Walmart's processes resulted in a low-cost, high-volume trustworthy brand for its customers. Apple's focus on designing a unique physical experience set it apart from competitors. Today, becoming a resilient organization means you will need to constantly innovate within multiple focus areas.

Reflect on the following eight dimensions of your business model to come up with ideas of what you might transform or improve. Write down every single idea that comes to mind.

- Positioning
- Product
- Pricing
- Promotion
- Place (distribution)
- Physical experience
- Processes
- People

At this stage, focus on quantity rather than quality of ideas. Remember, your competitor most likely only has three ideas. In our Outthinker workshops, it's common that leadership teams generate close to 200 ideas. After completing this exercise, you'll have a reservoir of strategic options from which to choose ideas to focus on now and, even better, to return to when you need to adjust.

## 4. Analyze

Now that you have a long list of ideas, the next challenge is to choose which ones you will execute. Your goal is to help reach strategic clarity and define your game plan. Rather than asking yourself: "Which ideas could I see working?" which can lead to repeating obvious and familiar strategies from the past, consider every idea and rate it based on the following two characteristics:

- *Ease:* Will this idea be easy or difficult to execute?
- *Impact:* If I had a magic wand and could execute this idea immediately, would it have a big or small impact?

The goal is to find a way to win with the least amount of effort and the greatest amount of ease.

Through this process, you will sort all of your ideas into four types of ideas:

- **Tactics:** Ideas that are easy to execute, but will not significantly improve your situation. You may want to execute these, but they are not big enough to put on your priority list.
- **Wastes of time:** These are low-impact and difficult to achieve. You should remove these from your agenda, because they are probably wasting resources. We often find that, through this exercise, companies identify many initiatives that are time wasters.
- **Winning moves:** These are high-impact ideas that are easy to execute. You should probably begin acting on these ideas immediately. They are inexpensive, low risk, quick to execute, and can have a major positive impact on your game.
- **Crazy ideas:** These appear difficult to achieve but could lead to significant strides. Most companies reject these ideas because they are too hard to execute. Innovative companies, by contrast, keep these ideas alive. They do not execute them right away, but they continue to discuss them, looking for ways to improve their achievability in the future.

Choose three to seven ideas that you will act or experiment on to validate. Don't get rid of the other ideas you've plotted; hold onto the complete list. You will maintain a healthy *ecosystem* of ideas that are constantly competing with one another. In the near future, you may find that something that seemed like a tactic becomes a winning move. For example, before the COVID-19 crisis, Airbnb had shifted its focus to acquiring new users as a run up to its initial public offering. During the pandemic, realizing its historical focus on providing connection and building a strong host community was the company's true competitive advantage, the company pivoted to dedicate resources to fully support its hosts.

Sometimes a winning move becomes a waste of time. For Outthinker, when the pandemic hit, in-person speaking completely dried up. We were forced to return to our list of ideas. For years, organizing an event had always been a backburner, crazy idea; but with many speakers, thought leaders, and guests stuck at home, hosting a virtual event became a winning move. We quickly shifted and launched two virtual conferences with some of the top business thinkers, including Scott Anthony, Tiffani Bova, Amy Edmonson, and Daniel

Pink, among others. As a result, we ended up raising over US$150,000 for COVID-19 charities and built a new virtual studio to deliver online speeches, workshops, and training.

Once you've built your list of 50 to 200 ideas, when a disruptive situation occurs, you won't need to come up with all new ideas. You'll come back to your original list, consider the new reality, and choose the best ideas for the circumstances.

## 5. Sell

The fifth step, Sell, will be in the background as you progress through the entire IDEAS process. A strategy that people do not understand or believe in is one they will not act on. So it's essential that you sell the strategy to build buy-in and support. Although presented as a final step in the IDEAS process, this is actually an ongoing conversation across your team and organization, and you'll need to practice it continuously. Sadly, many great ideas fail because the person who presents them cannot sell them effectively to their organization, investors, employees, and so forth. You can combat this by engaging the necessary stakeholders early and often.

You'll want to think strategically about how you deliver your message. We suggest a four-step sequence to define the influence you want to have. We call this process GAME:

- Goal: What do you want to achieve?
- Audience: Whom do you need to influence?
- Message: What do you want to say?
- Engagement: How will you engage them in the message?

Research shows that most effective innovators view this political process as an exciting challenge rather than a frustrating obstacle. The greatest leaders understand the power of influence and how to focus that influence on the right stakeholder, deliver a carefully designed message, and support it with a convincing argument. Sell is more than the final step. It's the glue that comes from turning the strategic conversation into an ongoing, living dialogue. It will become embedded in the shared language that forms your team and organization's cultures and behaviors.

## Conclusion

This is a brief overview of a five-step process that has taken about two decades to refine. If you analyze why Amazon, Apple, and Netflix are still around but in a reinvented state, you will see that they were able to adapt to change because within their organizations they continually have all five conversations. They are imagining the future, dissecting their business models, expanding their options, analyzing and prioritizing options, and continually selling their evolving strategies internally to make sure everyone joins the journey. When put into practice, this process has helped companies generate over US$2.5 billion in new recurring revenue while surviving strategic shifts that demand great resilience. In the newly released edition of *Outthink the Competition*, we walk through each of these steps in much greater detail (Krippendorff, 2022).

The practice of working through the IDEAS process creates a framework for resilience. Once you've completed the steps above, you will have already assessed your business model, generated somewhere around 200 ideas, and plotted a portfolio matrix. When you need to readjust for any reason, you won't need to start from ground zero. Instead, return to the five steps, look at your list of ideas, and plot a new course from there. With a process that is built to transform and adapt, you can find ease in knowing that change was always part of the plan.

## Reference

Krippendorff, K. (2022). *Outthink the competition* (2nd ed.). Wiley.

## About the Authors

**Kaihan Krippendorff** began his career with McKinsey & Company before founding growth strategy and innovation consulting firm Outthinker. Recognized by Thinkers50 as one of the top eight innovation thought leaders in the world, he is the author of five best sellers, most recently the Edison Award nominated, *Driving Innovation from Within: A Guide for Internal Entrepreneurs*. Amid a dizzying schedule of keynote speeches, consulting projects, and ongoing research, Kaihan finds time to teach at business schools globally (including New York University and Florida International University), write regularly for *Fast Company* and other major media outlets, and play an active role on four corporate advisory boards.

**Cori Dombroski** directs marketing for Outthinker and manages the member experience for the Outthinker Strategy Network. Her professional background includes leading Channel Enablement and Partner Marketing for IBM Data & Analytics segments and producing content for the Growth Institute's Scaling Up courses. She has also been a teacher of language and literature who continues to be passionate about education, storytelling, and connecting communities of inspired individuals.

# Built to Morph: Generative Capacity in the Protean Age

JEFFREY KUHN

# 13

It was a Kodak moment like no other. On 19 January 2012, Eastman Kodak, the storied firm synonymous with photography, filed for bankruptcy protection, yet another victim of the Digital Age. As quickly as you can say c-h-e-e-s-e, selfies and *gramming* (posting photos taken with a smartphone on Instagram) had rendered its mighty photography empire obsolete, a historical footnote. Like Icarus, the erstwhile Dow 30 firm had soared to great heights, only to come crashing back to earth, its wings scorched by profound technological and consumer shifts that had given rise to new, digital competitors playing by a different set of rules.

There have been countless postmortems concerning Kodak's fall from grace. Most commentaries point to common organizational pathologies, from hubris and denial to overharvesting its dying film business and its comfy, paternalistic culture that left the firm soft and uncompetitive. Its precipitous collapse, however, was several decades in the making. As the industry standard-bearer, Kodak was a prime target for competitors and regulators alike. Over the years, it had been bruised by a succession of body blows, from antitrust litigation to a series of frontal assaults mounted by Fujifilm, Polaroid, and digital photography, which it had ironically invented in its own research labs in 1975. The knockout blow, however, came from a decisive left hook landed by Apple's iPhone—Silicon Valley's equivalent to Mike Tyson—which dropped Kodak to the mat.

Reflecting on his experience in leading Kodak through the valley of death, former CEO Antonio Pérez (2005–2014) framed Kodak's transformation challenge as a metamorphosis:

> I use the term metamorphosis. It's a combination of things. In an animal body, a large number of cells will have to die, and completely new cells will have to be created. And these new cells must be very different from the ones that die, and all this has to be done at the same time. (Perez, 2015)

Hindsight is of course 20/20, but it is nonetheless refreshing to hear an executive frame a transformation in biological terms, rather than Newtonian mechanics, which, regrettably, is the dominant paradigm in many organizations.

## Brace for Turbulence

Ever since Igor Ansoff, the father of strategic management, introduced the concept of *environmental turbulence* into the strategic lexicon more than four decades ago, organizations have experimented with novel organizational forms and management practices—from honeycomb organizations to moving fast and breaking things—to get ahead of the curve and adapt faster to abrupt market shifts.

Nowadays, idiosyncrasy is a prized strategic asset. But this wasn't always the case. If we were to travel back in time—say 100 years—we would encounter a much different organizational milieu, influenced by the mechanistic writings of Max Weber (bureaucracy), Frederick W. Taylor (scientific management), and Henri Fayol (administrative theory). Their screeds echoed the prevailing cosmology of an orderly, Newtonian universe that ran with clocklike precision, in which inputs equaled outputs, actions produced reactions, and big problems could be broken down into small pieces that could be analyzed in isolation.

The Newtonian worldview suited early 20th century organizations well. Markets were relatively stable and predictable and evolved in an incremental, linear manner; industries were composed of a handful of dominant players that competed on the basis of size and structural advantage (think sumo wrestling); and management systems centered on the holy trinity of reducing variance (and, thereby, cost), optimizing assets, and maximizing output, with little concern for helping employees achieve their full potential, the so-called *soft* stuff.

The stifling bureaucracies and dehumanizing management systems of yesteryear are a far cry from today's informal, human-centered firms in which employees are asked to bring their *whole selves*—even their pets—to loft-like workplaces decked out with bean bag chairs, foosball tables, yoga studios, and tony espresso bars. But in the early years of the 20th century, the prescriptions offered by Weber et al. laid the foundation for decades of unprecedented economic prosperity and a burgeoning middle class.

In the 1950s, at the dawn of the Information Age, the tectonic plates began to shift as paradigm-busting discoveries in quantum physics and complexity theory gradually displaced Newton's orderly universe. The mechanistic worldview of the Industrial Age had outlived its usefulness as the business landscape became more dynamic and uncertain. Firms no longer jousted in insulated provincial markets but in unstructured global arenas with new players and new rules. Facing growing strategic intensity and market complexity, leaders—and their organizations—began to embody more fluid modes of thinking and being, shapeshifting from well-oiled machines into living organisms nestled within broader socioeconomic ecosystems.

In the 1990s, the twin forces of globalization and digitization eroded long-standing barriers to entry, giving rise to new types of competitors and ways of organizing economic activity and creating customer value. Armed with a growing arsenal of digital weaponry, companies kicked into high gear, shifting the basis of competition from sumo wrestling to mixed-martial arts. Firms could no longer rely on linear flywheel- and hedgehog-based strategies to sustain market leadership—network effects and exponential growth curves were the new kids on the block.

The Protean Age had arrived. And companies soon realized that they were competing in a Tesla world with Model T management systems. Organizational resilience, renewal, reinvention, and regeneration had come of age.

## Teaching Elephants to Dance

For decades, a debate has raged in professordom regarding whether elephants can dance, meaning: Can large, established firms innovate and create the markets and industries of tomorrow, or are they hamstrung by their obsessive pursuit of efficiency and defense of their core business? On one side of the debate, a spate of scholars have concluded that it is nearly impossible to be both *large* and *innovative*: the bigger the firm, the smaller the thinking, they reason. Citing compelling evidence, they argue that most market-creating innovations are launched by stealthy newcomers from outside the industry, not industry incumbents (think Apple's ambush on Nokia and BlackBerry with its iPhone). Why? Established firms lack the mindsets and skill sets to imagine the products, customers, and markets of tomorrow. Their strengths lie elsewhere— in defending and extending existing businesses. When breakthrough innovations do occur, such as Ken Kutaragi's oft-cited Herculean effort in launching the Sony PlayStation, it is cast as an act of sedition led by a gaggle of gray-haired revolutionaries and corporate malcontents who, under cover of darkness, bring the fabled offering to market.

The elephants-can't-dance narrative has dominated the innovation discourse since the early 1990s when 20th century firms struggled to retool their enterprises for the Digital Age. In the Industrial Era, time was an ally. The future looked a lot like the past, and organizations could incrementally adapt to changes in the market landscape with little concern of being disrupted. Like their brethren roaming the savannas of Africa, the corporate pachyderms of the Industrial Era leveraged their heft to mark their territory and stomp out would-be competitors.

However, as competitive intensity increased and commoditization cycles accelerated, executives began to recognize that harvesting their core businesses ad infinitum was no longer a tenable strategy. A dual operating system was needed to defend and extend the core business while simultaneously incubating and commercializing next-generation businesses that augment (and often attack) the core. Cleaving the organization into separate businesses based on their maturity and strategic posture (i.e., defend and extend versus incubate and attack) provided a vehicle for companies to be big and innovative. Elephants had found a way to dance.

Organizational ambidexterity, as it is called, is an intriguing concept on paper, but instituting antipodal organizational systems raises a raft of thorny questions. For instance, can defend-and-extend and incubate-and-attack businesses peacefully coexist under the same roof? If yes, how do you insulate embryonic incubate-and-attack businesses from pernicious organizational antibodies? What about leadership? Can operationally oriented managers who spent the bulk of their careers optimizing the core business suddenly channel their inner Elon Musk? And here's a biggie that few dare to ask: Why cleave an organization into warring tribes in the first place? Why not just turn the entire organization into a big, mean innovation machine that morphs its way into the future?

## It Takes ~~a Village~~ an Ecosystem

"Do you know what my favorite renewable fuel is? An ecosystem for innovation."
—Thomas Friedman

In 1961, Burns and Stalker noted that firms operating in stable environments tend to establish mechanistic, top-down managerial systems with regimented roles and responsibilities, whereas firms in more turbulent environments deploy flatter, more informal organizations staffed by generalists (Burns & Stalker, 1961). Today, few stable environments exist. Most industries are in a constant state of flux—it is difficult to identify a company today that is not being buffeted by turbulence.

To create adaptive enterprises that are built to morph, firms increasingly are drawing inspiration from a range of sources, from Darwin to democracies to markets, and even food—anything but machines. W. L. Gore, Alphabet, Apple, and Amazon are often held up as exemplars of this new organizational ethos, which, at first blush resembles a mosh pit more than a commercial enterprise. But beneath this frat party veneer lies a host of organizational design elements that must be carefully considered and orchestrated, such as the degree of decentralization, autonomy, self-organization, modularity, boundary permeability, human diversity (cognitive, educational, and life experience), and the collaborative mechanisms needed to gain an evolutionary advantage.

## Oticon's Spaghetti Organization

Long before Jeff Bezos issued his two-pizza decree (project teams should be small enough to be fed with two pizzas) there was Oticon's spaghetti organization. In 1990, the Danish hearing-aid manufacturer introduced an amorphous organizational model that took a wrecking ball to the company's hierarchy, abolishing formal reporting relationships, job titles, and assigned offices and desks, empowering employees to exercise the law of two feet and choose the projects they wished to contribute to or lead.

Arriving at Oticon as CEO in 1988 to revitalize the ailing company, Lars Kolind (1988–1998) spent the first two years of his tenure trimming excess fat to get the firm in fighting shape (Kolind, 2006). In 1990, with Oticon in the black, Kolind realized that more radical steps were needed to compete with better-resourced firms that had leapfrogged Oticon. "We had to find something that we could do in a unique fashion," he said. "That led me to believe that if we could design a uniquely innovative, fast-moving, efficient organization, then this is something they [Oticon's competitors] could never replicate."

Kolind was inspired by his volunteer work with the Boy Scouts; he marveled at the way troopers from all walks of life came together and cooperated on projects without a hierarchy. "There was no game-playing, no intrigue; we are one family brought together through common goals," he said. His experiences in the Scout movement led him to cultivate a compelling organizational purpose for Oticon grounded in self-motivation and supporting others.

The spaghetti organization was unsettling at first to the structured, time-conscious Danes with staffers jetting from project to project with their rolling workstations, but the organization eventually found its groove. True to form, though, over time, long-standing project teams hardened into quasi departmental tribes; Kolind found himself having to reshuffle teams periodically to prevent stasis from creeping in.

## Planting Banyan Trees at Haier

Companies like to tout their Darwinian bona fides, but when it comes to creating a self-renewing enterprise built to morph, Chinese multinational Haier is in a league of its own. Over the past four decades, the firm has undergone a remarkable metamorphosis from a conventional white-goods manufacturer to an ecosystem-based enterprise encompassing a labyrinth of digitally enabled businesses, from smart cities to education and healthcare. The firm's unique propagation-based growth model has germinated an autopoietic ecology of entrepreneurial microenterprises (small autonomous business units) that spawn a steady stream of edgy, new-to-the-world businesses that continuously regenerate the enterprise and propel it into the future.

Haier's mighty herd of microenterprises (there are legions of them) set their own strategies, make decisions independently without first gaining approval from higher-ups (there are no middle managers at Haier), elect their own leaders, hire—and fire—team members, procure services from internal or external providers, and determine their own compensation. In true Darwinian fashion, market-facing microenterprises are required to secure external funding—an important market signal—and invest personal funds in their venture so they have ample skin in the game and can realize a financial upside. In the event a microenterprise is unable to secure external venture capital or advance customer orders, the business is deemed unviable and must fend for itself without a financial lifeline from Haier.

I had the honor of visiting Haier's global headquarters in Qingdao, China, to interview a cross-section of microenterprises and senior executives, including former CEO Zhang Ruimin. On the first morning of my visit, my translator and I paused in the lobby of Haier's executive building to admire a magnificent banyan tree growing in a 20-foot-wide planter. She explained that banyan trees are a symbol of immortality in Eastern culture, and that Haier recognizes a select group of microenterprises each year for entrepreneurial excellence with its coveted Golden Banyan award.

Banyan trees have remarkable regenerative properties. They self-propagate through an aerial root system that sprouts new roots and trunks when their downward-growing branches touch the ground, expanding the tree's footprint in unpredictable ways. To put this into perspective, the Great Banyan near Kolkata, India, has more than 4,000 root-cum-trunk structures that collectively create a 156,000-square-foot canopy that from a distance looks like a forest.

The mythical banyan tree is more than a cultural symbol at Haier; it is a talisman for life itself. As I listened to Haier executives describe the organization's growth model, I quickly realized that they were operating from a different worldview. Unlike Western leaders, who frame business growth in terms of s-curves; two-by-two grids; and narrow addressable markets, Haier's leaders view growth as a boundless, propagation-based process governed by the laws of nature, as signified by the sprawling banyan tree.

As Haier's microenterprise model matured, Zhang observed a powerful synergy between its mushrooming network of microenterprises and the Internet of Things (IoT) era, the contours of which were beginning to form. In this new era, he concluded, competition would be among ecosystems and ecosystem brands for lifelong users (end customers); Haier would cocreate value with users through the ecosystems it orchestrated. In 2019, the firm embarked on an ecosystem-based strategy to create a curated, interactive relationship with end customers. As its ecosystems took root, Haier's products became mediums through which users could cocreate unique personalized experiences with a community of ecosystem partners, creating a cycle of increasing returns for both Haier and its partners. To support its strategy, Haier recast its platform structure as a constellation of ecosystem-based businesses, creating an internal organizational landscape that mirrored the connectedness and dynamism of the external environment. Zhang likened his role as CEO to that of an ecologist, "creating favorable conditions and mechanisms for species in the Haier ecosystem to prosper on their own in a sustainable way." (Zhang, 2021)

## Accelerating Darwin: From Adaptation to Preemption

As exemplified in the Oticon and Haier examples, organizations have made great strides over the past several decades reconceptualizing themselves as ecological systems rather than machines. This new zeitgeist has unleashed the entrepreneurial *élan* of employees, producing a level of serendipity unimaginable a century ago, and creating enterprises that are highly adaptive to exogeneous rumblings.

The ecological systems perspective provides countless benefits to businesses, but there is a vast difference between adapting to the future when it arrives and having the generative capacity to create it. Organizations that rely solely on incremental, sense-and-adapt-type evolution often find themselves playing a perpetual game of catch-up. Steady organizational evolution is paramount, but it must be combined with bold, unconventional strategies that are difficult for competitors to decode and imitate. To accelerate Darwin, organizational *evolution* and strategic *revolution* must be pursued simultaneously.

As an author, I am always on the lookout from an incisive story to share with business leaders. A few years ago, I listened to an interview with the head coach of the Cleveland Browns (an American football team) in which he described the dramatic increase in the speed of play in the National Football League (NFL) compared with collegiate football and his efforts in helping his first-year quarterback expand his *picture book* of offensive-defensive formations and maneuvers to heighten his ability to recognize patterns and accelerate his execution of plays. Later in the interview, the coach observed that as the fledgling quarterback expanded his picture book throughout the season, the game began to slow down for him; meaning, as the quarterback's ability to recognize patterns sped up, his perception of the speed of play slowed down, enabling him to see a range of emerging scenarios in his mind's eye even before they happened.

Similarly, when executives develop a repertoire of strategic patterns (their competitive picture book), their perception of the speed of play decelerates, and the future begins to unfold in slow motion, creating opportunities for preemption. In business, we call this *strategic sensemaking*, a cognitive capability that requires sophisticated pattern recognition and strategic thinking skills.

Kodak wasn't blindsided by the future. It had plenty of advance notice concerning the epochal shift from film to digital imaging but failed to refresh its picture book (its mental models) and compose an exciting tableau of the future in its viewfinder. Like many of its Industrial Era counterparts, Kodak struggled to adapt to the speed of play of the Digital Age and lacked the generative capacity—both cognitive and organizational—to conceive bold, new businesses that expand the vistas of possibility.

Just think, had Kodak been built to morph, we would be posting selfies and pictures of banyan trees on Kodagram, instead of Instagram.

## References

Burns, T., & Stalker, G. M. (1961). *The management of innovation*. Tavistock.

Kolind, L. (2006). *The second wave: Winning the war against bureaucracy*. Wharton School Publishing.

Perez, A. (2015). *The big bankruptcy at Eastman Kodak*. YouTube Video. https://www.youtube.com/watch?v=B_S64FjPlD4

Zhang, R. (2021). *Zhang Ruimin discusses IoT and Life X.O*. Internal memorandum. Haier Group Cultural Industry Ecosystem.

## About the Author

**Dr. Jeffrey Kuhn** is an executive advisor and educator focused on enterprise strategy, leadership, and transformation. His work centers on helping senior business leaders develop the capacity to think and lead strategically in dynamic market environments undergoing profound change. He holds a doctorate from Columbia University and has served on the faculty of Columbia Business School.

# Achieving Resilience Through Structural and Systems Change

DAVID LIDDLE

# 14

The challenges of the past few years have pushed the subject of organizational resilience right to the top of the boardroom agenda. Faced with the fallout from the COVID-19 pandemic, the war in Ukraine, and increasingly pressing social and environmental challenges, senior leaders have been tussling with everything from the resilience of their product or service offering and how well their supply chain is holding up, through to the breakdown of employee trust and pressing skills shortages.

What's interesting is that most of the conversations that have been taking place have focused on operational resilience. The emphasis has been on the business continuity plan, the need for the organization to manage risk effectively and to develop the agility it needs to respond to changing markets and difficult situations.

What is less often discussed is the culture and climate that underpin the very foundations of this organizational resilience. You can have the best business continuity plan in the world, but if working environments are toxic, the core values and purpose are unclear and employees feel unheard and undervalued, the plan isn't worth the paper it's written on.

If organizations are to achieve real, lasting resilience, nothing short of a full-scale structural and systems change is needed. The change must address everything from leadership, values, and purpose through to the way people are managed on the frontline; how HR policies and processes are framed; and how workplace conflict, complaints, and concerns are dealt with.

## What do We Mean by Resilience?

It's worth thinking about what we actually mean when we express a desire to build a resilient organization. Often, this is framed as the company's ability to survive in the face of adversity—to adapt and keep going in the face of challenges like the COVID-19 pandemic, for example, or to keep its head above water when shortages of parts or labor make it difficult to fulfill contracts or meet customer demand.

Organizations that are focused on truly transforming their culture, however, have the potential to go beyond this and make resilience a core competitive advantage. They are able to build the happy, healthy, and harmonious workplaces that result in maximum performance and productivity, and give them the agility they need to see the next opportunity and steal a march on their rivals.

However, too often, in their attempts to become resilient, organizations take a short-term, sticking plaster approach. They address the symptoms, rather than looking at bigger underlying causes of their lack of resilience.

## What Does a Resilient Organization Look Like?

In my book *Transformational Culture: Develop a People-Centred Organization for Improved Performance*, I describe the key dimensions of an agile and resilient organization, and outline the issues leaders need to address to achieve the people-centered, values-driven culture that will enable them to thrive rather than just survive.

For an organization to achieve true resilience, the following seven dimensions (seen in Figure 1) need to run like a golden thread through everything the business says and does.

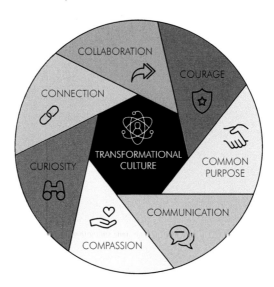

**Figure 1.** The 7Cs of a transformational culture.

**Courage:** Leaders and human resources (HR) professionals need the courage to cope with the changes and challenges of the future and to create conditions where the individual brilliance of employees is allowed to shine through. In practice, this means they need the courage to challenge the conventional wisdom that policies should come before people, and the courage to challenge the orthodoxies of control, power, and privilege. They need the courage to reform the systems and structures that feed inequality, division, and discord, and the courage to value sustainability and social justice as measures of a successful organization. Finally, they need the courage to resolve differences with empathy, dialogue, and understanding and to seek insight and wisdom from others, even those with whom they may disagree.

**Connection:** In a resilient organization, the connection among purpose, values, behaviors, and people is paramount. Top leaders recognize that they need to create flow between the culture and the climate of their organization. For this to occur, values and purpose must connect and be fully integrated into the corporate strategy and the overarching strategic narrative of the organization. The company's processes (policies, procedures, and rules) should connect with the purpose and the values. These processes should balance the needs and aspirations of the workforce with those of the business. The processes of the organization are the central pivot point of cultural flow (see Figure 2)—they provide the vital connection between climate and culture.

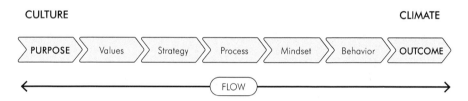

Figure 2. The culture flow system.

**Collaboration:** Working cooperatively and collaboratively is a fundamental feature of a resilient organization. Collaboration allows diverse and divergent views to be aired and discussed. This diversity of thinking and viewpoints may initiate some early tension but, when that tension is managed courageously, the different viewpoints can begin to yield fresh insights, creativity, and innovation. The problem with working collaboratively is that we are often afraid of the initial tension and do not feel confident enough to break through it to begin to secure the benefits of collaboration.

**Common Purpose:** Purpose is essential to creating energy, pride, and passion. It motivates each of us to achieve optimal performance and it underpins our efforts to work in collaboration with others. Common purpose comes through a connection with our values, which unites us in a single, coherent objective. You can see it, you can feel it, and you can almost touch it. Great customer service, happy employees filled with passion and pride—these are all the outward signs of an organization with common purpose. Achieving a common purpose does not mean we all agree; it does, however, mean that when we disagree, we disagree well. Common purpose allows disparate views to be aired and heard. It can be the source of a deeper understanding of problems, cooperative solution design, and the maximization of creativity and innovation.

**Communication:** Communication is a core feature of an agile and resilient organization—and a culture that is values based and person centered. When communication breaks down, the impact can be significant and severe. It can result in an erosion of trust and can undermine respect and damage morale. It is easy enough to communicate when targets are being hit and everyone is getting along well. It is much tougher, yet much more important, to communicate when we are tense, when we disagree, and when we are under stress. That is why dialogue—the ability to communicate as adults, with care, compassion, and understanding—has primacy in a resilient organization. The best communicators I have observed display humility, are authentic, and are safe with their own and other's vulnerabilities. They know how to frame dialogue so that they can learn from the past, understand the present, and work together to improve the future.

**Compassion:** Research has shown that if people are treated with compassion, they are more likely to stay in the organization longer and work harder for their employer. In the workplace, one of the greatest expressions of compassion is the action of our managers and leaders to resolve our quarrels and disagreements, and the action of HR to reduce the heavy toll of their retributive systems of justice. Compassion can also be shown through the policies and processes of our organization. It is no longer possible to describe oneself as a compassionate or humane manager, leader, or HR professional—while also continuing to deploy the stress-inducing and relationship-wrecking performance management and disciplinary and grievance procedures that still exist in most organizations today. True compassion will be achieved when our organizations rid themselves of these policy frameworks, and instead systematize empathy, dialogue, mutual respect and restorative, rather than retributive, justice.

**Curiosity:** Curiosity is one of the foundations of a healthy team and a healthy person. Yet we are often afraid to be curious about emotions and how people are feeling at work. Opening a dialogue about feelings creates a powerful bond of empathy and seeds deeper levels of insight and understanding. Being curious and asking questions allows people to be vulnerable in a safe place and acts as a basis for building trust and establishing psychological safety. If we want to improve employees' mental health, make workplaces safer, and reduce the incidence of stress and stress-related absence, we could start by encouraging our managers and leaders to be a little bit more curious about people. They need to be reassured that it is okay to ask employees how they are feeling. Curious people know that inviting the other person to talk opens both of their minds to new possibilities and new opportunities.

## Key Questions to Ask About the 7Cs

1. Do your leaders have the necessary capabilities and strategic impetus to create and sustain these 7Cs?
2. Do your HR policies and procedures promote these 7Cs?
3. Do your performance and reward systems value and encourage the 7Cs?
4. Do your line managers enact these 7Cs through their daily Actions, Interactions, and Reactions (the AIR our managers breathe out, which creates the climate of our teams)?

## How to Get There

So if these are the tenets of a truly resilient organization, what do leaders need to do to create space for them to emerge and to truly embed them? In *Transformational Culture*, I set out a model (see Figure 3), which can act as a blueprint for building a resilient and agile culture. The model is a blend of interconnected elements that span an organization's entire ecosystem. It can be used to support the process of designing, implementing, and sustaining the changes that will lead to a fair, just, inclusive, sustainable, and resilient culture. The application of the model is supported through enhanced people processes, management systems, and leadership strategies and behaviors. While offering a framework, it is not prescriptive and can be adapted and flexed to meet the organization's unique sector, maturity, context, needs, and circumstances. These are some of the key areas organizations need to focus on if they want to make a real difference In their level of resilience.

**Figure 3.** Transformational culture model.

### Aligning Purpose and Values

Values are the golden thread that run through an organization. They bind a transformational culture together by aligning an organization's purpose and strategy with its agreed behaviors and overall customer and employee experience. The values of your organization are perhaps one of its greatest commodities and should be carefully developed, designed, and integrated across the fabric of the business.

Values cannot be superficial PR statements or inconsequential jargon, which has no relevance to people's everyday working lives. Those are not values—those are words stuck on a lobby wall. It is vital we do not get the two mixed up.

Successful organizations understand that their values are a key part of their brand and reputation. They can create powerful connections between employees and between an organization and its stakeholders and its investors—values such as creating an inclusive workplace, treating people with respect, being fair and just in the way we solve problems, celebrating our diversity, and acting in a way that is sustainable and reduces our impact on the planet.

Values, at their best, are empowering and evoke a sense of common purpose across even the most disparate business. They generate a sense of belonging and provide a powerful system by which we can hold ourselves, and others, to account. They are the basis for us to build trust, mutual respect, and confidence. Having a clearly defined and widely owned set of values is one of the important elements of a transformational culture—and of a high-performing, agile, and resilient organization.

## Integrating Transformational Justice

We need a radical shift in the way our organizations think about justice. Justice is at the heart of a civilized society, but the question we need to ask is: Do the rules, procedures, and policies commonly used in organizations actually deliver justice? You only have to look at the increasing number of headlines about toxic workplace cultures to see that the answer is a resounding no.

We are still reliant on damaging and divisive disciplinary, grievance, and performance management policies that do more harm than good. They encourage a right/wrong, win/lose, shame/blame mindset, pitting people against one another in stress-inducing procedures that result in relationships (and people) being irrevocably damaged.

These retributive models of justice creep around in organizations like a thief in the night, causing untold damage and destruction. Their sheer existence invokes an adversarial and confrontational mindset and dynamic in teams, departments, and across entire organizations. Engagement declines, absence levels rocket, productivity takes a nosedive, and talented people leave. No one wins.

Transformational justice is a new model of justice that balances the rules of the organization, the rights of the employee, and the need to generate fair, just, and inclusive outcomes when things go wrong. At its core, it is about reducing harm, building trust, protecting relationships, promoting psychological safety, and creating opportunities for insight, reflection, and learning.

## Turning HR into a People and Culture Function

If organizations are going to adopt the kind of transformational culture that will help them build resilience, the human resources function must take urgent action to become purpose, people, and values led. HR must transform itself into an overarching people and culture function and needs to make moves to release itself from the burden of its perceived proximity to management. The term *business partner*, for example, is a divisive and loaded term that results in HR being perceived by many as the long arm of management. This perception of systemic bias impedes the effectiveness of HR and erodes trust in its role and its systems. If HR is to remain a trusted and effective function in the organization, it must rise above the paradigms of power, hierarchy, and control. It must focus on becoming a catalyst for world-class customer experience (CX) and should be the function within our organizations that connects employee experience (EX) with CX.

## Combining WEI into a Single Overarching Strategic Narrative

The way we currently think about well-being, engagement, and inclusion (WEI) within our organizations is not working. Yet the impact of COVID-19 on our mental health, the rise of social and employee activism, and the increased focus on employee experience have made these areas of the workplace some of the most discussed and hotly debated topics of our times.

It is my firm belief that if we approach WEI as a single strategic narrative within our organizations, we will achieve a much clearer focus on employee experience and will be further down the path toward developing a culture that puts its purpose and its people first.

It is not rocket science to figure out that a happier, healthier, and harmonious workforce leads to high performance and better employee experience. There is a clear interface between an inclusive workplace, where people can shine and be brilliant, are supported by their managers, and feel enhanced levels of engagement as a result. However, delivering this great human and employee experience, coupled with world-class customer experience, requires planning, resourcing, and dedication—as well as unflinching leadership to ensure that WEI remains a central focus for the organization.

It also requires systems-based thinking, rather than the one-size-fits-all, siloed approach, which is sadly all too common. Organizations currently watch the three elements of well-being, engagement, and diversity, equity and inclusion swimming down separate lanes and invest money and resources into each, without stepping back to look at them in totality. They analyze predictable annual employee-engagement results. They ask "why aren't you engaged?" rather than taking a wider systemic look at the entire organization and causal factors around managing conflict, having quality conversations about performance, creating psychologically safe and inclusive work and project teams, or dealing with mental health challenges in a joined-up way.

There is no magic bullet or simple answer to the big challenges of improving employee well-being, engagement, and inclusion. If there were, organizations would have solved the WEI puzzle long ago. The emergence of employee experience (EX) is a step in the right direction. However, unless EX can actively address the wider issues of WEI, it could easily just become another business fad. That is why organizations must, as a matter of urgency, become much better at measuring the visible and invisible forces that connect well-being, engagement, and inclusion.

## Addressing Leadership and Management Behaviors

The way in which a leader or manager behaves is perhaps the single biggest factor affecting organizational culture, leaving unwritten cues and clues for the rest of the workforce. The climate of a team, for example, can be characterized predominantly by the behaviors of its leaders and managers. The climate is particularly sensitive to the way leaders and managers **A**ct, **I**nteract, and **R**eact with one another, with employees, with suppliers, and with customers. The **AIR** that our leaders and managers produce through their behaviors becomes the air we all breathe in—it creates the climate we work in. This is more acute in times of stress brought on by conflict, change, or crisis. Then the AIR can become thick and choking; the climate can become toxic, destructive, and dysfunctional.

*Actions* are the day-to-day behaviors of the leader or manager. Aggressive, irritable, exclusive, divisive, or inconsistent behaviors can create and perpetuate a toxic climate. Day-to-day behaviors that are respectful, supportive, empowering, compassionate, and empathetic set the tone for a transformational climate and culture and a happy, healthy, and harmonious workplace.

*Interactions* describe the ways our leaders and managers engage and interact with others, verbally, in emails, on social media, or in meetings. Where those interactions are uncivil, disrespectful, misogynistic, blaming, shaming, or rude, those characteristics easily become the accepted behavioral norms. Where the interactions of leaders or managers are driven by a sense of personal responsibility and are people centered and values driven, they are setting the standard—giving an implicit license for others to follow suit.

*Reactions* describe how our managers and leaders respond during times of conflict, change, or crisis. During these times, like any human being, the leader or manager can expect to feel mixed emotions and will experience stress, anxiety, vulnerability, and confusion. We do not expect our leaders to be saints or robotic, but when feelings and emotions take over and the leader or manager loses their grip on them, their reactions to stress set the tone for others.

Our expectations of our leaders are changing at a blistering pace. The old orthodoxies of autocracy and rigidity, command and control, and power and hierarchy are being challenged. If they are to build resilience in business, leaders need to create a clear and compelling vision and proactively shape and reset the organization for the future. They need to build resilience so that they and their teams remain engaged, motivated, and creative. They must ensure that their organizations, divisions, and teams promote psychological safety, are inclusive, and that their managers possess the capability to manage conflict and change effectively.

As our organizations strive to become more resilient, the cultural orthodoxies of yesterday will not be sufficient to resolve the challenges of tomorrow. Adopting the kind of transformational culture I describe in this article will shape the future of the organization and accelerate its growth, ensuring that it is able to attract top talent, top investors, and top customers.

**About the Author**

**David Liddle** is CEO of the leading transformational culture consultancy, The TCM Group, and founding president of the Institute of Organizational Dynamics. He is the author of two books, *Managing Conflict* (Kogan Page/ CIPD, 2017), and *Transformational Culture: Develop a People-Centred Organization for Improved Performance* (Kogan Page, 2021).

# Leading Into an Unknown Future: Why Learning Organizations Prove Resilient, but Not Vice Versa

CARSTEN LINZ

15

G iven the current convolution of crisis, there is no doubt that organizations need to learn to operate in the face of an unknown future with extremely uncertain conditions such as climate change; COVID-19; the Ukraine conflict; massive inflation; supply chain disruptions; transformative regulatory shifts, such as the European Union's green deal; cyberattacks; and moral and ethical dilemmas such as Google's artificial intelligence (AI) withdrawal from the Pentagon's military drone program. This also shows in numbers. The Global Economic Policy Uncertainty Index—a GDP-weighted average of national economic policy uncertainty (EPU) indices for 20 countries—has climbed from 76 in 1996 to 303 in March 2022 with a historical peak in May 2020 of 430 during the pandemic. (EPU, 2022)

Uncertainty means that the probabilities of the relevant environmental conditions occurring are unknown to the decision maker. Risk is a special case of uncertainty, namely with the probabilities at least known. (In the case of certainty, all parameters and goals are known with 100% probability.) Further, uncertainty is characterized by, first, the severity of changes; second, their frequency; and, third, the persistence of these abnormal or crisis situations. Uncertainty is by no means a new phenomenon; however, going forward, leaders will have to bring a fresh look at uncertainty.

At the peak of the pandemic Brian Chesky, Airbnb's CEO, explained the extreme uncertainty: "We don't know exactly when travel will return. When travel does return, it will look different." Today's conditions have triggered an increase in all parameters of the uncertainty complex and makes future developments nearly impossible to predict. Hence, companies need to prepare for the unexpected, build strategic options, and strengthen their capability to proactively shape the future instead of solely responding to it. With new and disruptive currents, this leadership challenge is here to stay.

## Resilience: The Pitfall of Treating it as a Means Instead of an Outcome

Recently, resilience has emerged as the central response to just about everything—both at the individual and organizational levels. However, resilience is an outcome, not a means, and the negative consequences can be significant when resilience is misunderstood as a means.

Defined as a person's psychological ability to adapt to stressful circumstances and recover from adverse events, regardless of circumstances and challenges, resilience is a highly sought-after personality skill in the modern workplace. Recently, there has been a tendency to transfer this individual trait to organizations and consider it as the ideal of a firm's capabilities.

But the opposite is true. If you make resilience the means, you can easily end up with toughness. History teaches us that leaders who strive for toughness should be critically observed. Toughness was declared a key trait and ideal in the Third Reich. To counteract an alleged effeminacy of youth, leaders were required to be "nimble as greyhounds, tough as leather, hard as Krupp steel." (Roddewig, 2022). Curiously absent from this pejorative *ideal* are all the classical virtues of the Age of Enlightenment such as learning, wisdom, and justice.

Numerous recent studies show that too much focus on resilience leads to a denial of the larger need to explore and heal situations (Pierce & Aguinis, 2013). For individuals, too much personal resilience can lead to being too tolerant of adversity, for example, staying too long in a toxic environment such as a demoralizing job. For companies, too much organizational resilience risks stressing organizations beyond what is reasonable.

Overly resilient leaders might satisfy the need of employees to be protected by a strong and tenacious leader; however, studies show that they can significantly reduce leadership effectiveness and, in turn, team and organizational effectiveness (Chamorro-Premuzic & Lusk, 2017). Bold leaders are unaware of their limitations and overestimate their leadership abilities and current performance, leading them to be rigidly and unreasonably resistant and closed to information that could be essential to remediating—or at least improving—behavioral weaknesses. The same holds true on an organizational level when endurance stands as an obstacle to learning.

While it may be reassuring for countries, organizations, and teams to select leaders based on their resilience, such leaders are not necessarily always good for the group or organization. Employees can burn out, organizations can fail to shape the future or even fail with immoral and unethical practices.

Learning organizations, on the other hand, win. When leaders make learning the means, organizations can intelligently deal with extreme uncertainty, proactively shape the future, adapt and evolve organizationally, and even stand the test of time or, in other words, achieve resilience as a by-product.

**"The key to pursuing excellence is to embrace an organic, long-term learning process, and not to live in a shell of static, safe mediocrity."**
—Josh Waitzkin

If business leaders are serious about building organizations that can stand the test of time, four actions will make the future better than we might think: (1) lead and learn with an infinite mindset, (2) develop options for strategic flexibility, (3) shift business models towards resilience, and (4) establish digital operating models for sensing organizations.

## Opportunity 1: Lead and Learn With an Infinite Mindset

**"We know that someone has won the game when all of the players have agreed who among them is the winner. No other condition than the agreement of the players is absolutely required in determining who has won the game."**—J.P. Carse

As we know, in business all of the players can determine their own strategies and tactics and there is no set of fixed rules on which everyone has agreed, other than the law and this can vary. Additionally, we may not know the other players, and new players can join the game at any time. Hence, it is surprising to see how many leaders still *play business* as if it were a finite game, namely, to win and beat the competition. But beating the competition is a losing business strategy.

Today, Siemens has evolved into an innovative company focused on growth through digitalization and sustainability, solving the most pressing problems to create a better future. The company was named "World Changing Company of the Year" in 2022 by *Fast Company* magazine (Toussaint, 2022). In contrast, in the 1980s and 1990s, Siemens focused primarily on competing directly with General Electric. This restructuring to beat the supposed role model came at the expense of the company's unique engineering culture, which had made it great and nearly made the company irrelevant.

Benchmarking never makes you better than your benchmark. Admiring worthy rivals can be motivating to constantly improve to stay in the game, but focusing on the competition defocuses innovation for the customer. Jeff Bezos wisely noted in the same context: "If we can get our competitors to focus on us while we focus on the customer, we'll end up right."

Instead, winners focus their leadership on a North Star, a transformative purpose, and long-term goals for people to embark on the journey to a greater cause. At Amazon, Jeff Bezos focused the long-term goal on "more products, cheaper, and faster" and kept reinvesting most of their cash into additional innovations.

Leading means changing. Changes in the environment should be followed by changes in the company, because entrepreneurial action is not an end in itself; rather, it serves to satisfy the needs of selected stakeholders. The harmonious fit between the conditions of the environment and the company's activities is closely linked to processes of organizational learning.

## Opportunity 2: Develop Options for Strategic Flexibility

When Steve Jobs said in his famous 2004 Stanford University commencement speech: "You can't connect the dots looking forward; you can only connect them looking backwards. So, you have to trust that the dots will somehow connect in your future," what he meant was that learning something *useless* in the short term can create an option that pays off in the future when the right application or use case emerges. In other words, thinking long term and learning a range of things increases the likelihood that the dots will connect later and *new combinations* can be enforced (Epstein, 2019).

Jobs was a leader, who naturally thought in terms of real options. Real options include derivatives that get their value from future decisions; they give the holder the right to make a decision in the future and involve real (i.e., physical) underlying assets. Real options can be understood as the acquisition of alternative courses of action, which enable specific activities to be carried out to secure opportunities and avoid threats as—through learning—further information is gained. They thus reflect the value of the additional flexibility gained.

Real options add the *wait* decision to the *invest* and *not invest* alternatives and take learning plus the resulting information gain into account, both passively and actively. This can lead to a change in course; for example, when an in-house development fails, then a development cooperation is sought instead. Since real options grant the right, but do not imply an obligation, to engage in certain activities, there is an asymmetry of opportunities for profit and risk of loss. Losses and expenses already incurred (sunk costs) can therefore be limited without restricting the realizable profit potential.

Especially in the face of high uncertainty, it is necessary to develop room for maneuvering at both the project and portfolio levels (Linz, 2000). The relationship between uncertainty and the required range of strategic options is also important. When uncertainty is high, the provision of a sufficiently large number of strategic options for action proves to be critical to success. As shown in Figure 1, the following applies: The greater the number of real options available to an organization, the greater the scope for action.

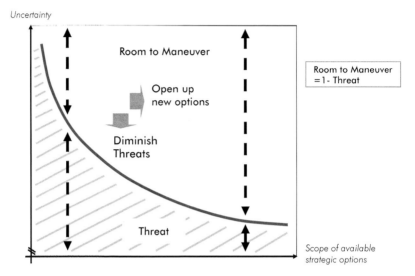

**Figure 1.** Room to maneuver depending on uncertainty and options.

Strategically, this implies a shift from high, largely irreversible investments in a few large projects (big bets) toward a portfolio of smaller investments into real options, hence room for maneuver. This allows the organization to reposition itself more quickly than competitors who concentrate on doing more of the same and being, therefore, resistant to change. It also reduces the risk that strategic windows cannot be exploited because specific resources and capabilities (sticky factors) are not available, and their development has already become too costly (lock-out). Such variant thinking places strategic focus on learning through experiments and fast feedback loops, and ultimately can transform an organization substantially.

We see that organizational slack can be a good thing to accelerate learning and increase an organization's strategic flexibility to stand the test of time. However, it is advisable to limit investments as not all options will be exercised. Hence, first develop an option with limited resources, then exercise and mobilize resources on a large scale only when competencies have been acquired, uncertainty has been reduced, and the strategic relevance is still considered to be high.

"Depending on the future environment, not all options will be exercised. However, those discarded are not wasted, but serve the useful purpose of insurance against an uncertain future."
—O.E. Williamson, 1999

This flexibility can even be existential. An existential flex, rather, happens when the company is fully formed and functioning. In this case, the leader is risking the apparent certainty of the current, profitable path with the uncertainty of a new path—one that could lead to the company's decline or even demise (Sinek, 2020). To the finite-minded leaders, such a move is not worth the risk.

To infinite-minded leaders, however, staying on the current path is the bigger risk. They embrace the uncertainty. Failure to flex, they believe, will significantly restrict their ability to advance the cause. They fear staying the course may even lead to eventual demise of the organization. The motivation of the infinite-minded player to flex is to advance the cause, even if it disrupts the existing business.

To build a learning organization, you need a leader who does not simply want to build an organization that can weather change but one that can be transformed by it. They want to build a company that embraces surprises, adapts with them, and comes out of times of upheaval entirely different than when they entered and are often grateful for the transformation. They embrace the surprise as an opportunity to transform for the better rather than a threat—a characteristic move of an infinite-minded leader.

To become great leaders, we must first be able to lead ourselves. If leaders can't change, the organization can't either (Linz, 2019).

## Opportunity 3: Shift Business Models Toward Resilience

We are witnessing the convergence of digital transformation, sustainability transformation, and business model transformation.

Digital technologies are the prerequisite for business impact as well as social impact at scale (Linz, 2022). However, many executives still view sustainability and technology as separate priorities and even opposing goals. But the opposite is true, as the interplay between digitalization and sustainability opens up brilliant opportunities for shaping a greener economy and society, and will change interpretation of the sustainability paradigm itself (International Institute, 2020).

But overhyping the deployment of digital technologies in existing businesses to do what we have always done, faster and cheaper, is not enough. If changes are too small, organizations run the risk of digitizing the past instead of innovating and transforming for the future.

Despite the reset on the horizon, many incumbent companies base their business models on yesterday's logic; they risk relying on improvements that only scratch the surface. Eighty percent of executives think that their business models are at risk, whereas 60% of companies that have successfully undergone a digital transformation say they have transformed into new business models (Corporate Leaders, 2019). To take full advantage of the opportunity priovided by crisis, we need to challenge our basic assumptions about how to create, deliver, and capture value.

Our analysis of 250 digital initiatives worldwide reveals that most companies still focus on *process automation* and efficiency gains (Linz et al., 2021). In other words, they make the existing processes more digital such as document workflows replacing paper-based processes.

Fortunately, an increasing number can be classified as *process reimagination* that challenges and puts the existing processes to the test before reimplementing them. Predictive maintenance scenarios replacing traditional repair–replace processes would fall into this category.

Only a minority of organizations *transform the operating model*, which implies that digital technologies have become an integral part of the organization's value-creation architecture. One example is Adidas group's so-called "Speedfactory" approach, which integrates a number of trends transforming supply chains today, including 3D printing, customization on a mass scale, near-sourcing, and the digitalization of its operations. Similarly, a bank that establishes a hub to provide financial services at other banks, or embeds them into enterprise processes, could be classified as an operating model transformation. Or the Circular Footware Alliance, which aims to produce a fully recyclable safety shoe made from recycled materials that can also be recycled after use.

Lastly, the smallest share of companies drives digital transformation in the form of a *business model transformation*. For example, Microsoft transformed from the Windows-grounded software product firm into a cloud platform company, which works across technologies and integrates with partners and ecosystems such as LinkedIn and GitHub. From 2015 to 2020, their share price has nearly quadrupled, and their revenues have grown by 65% and shifted from upfront licenses to recurring subscription revenues. Or EspeRare, a not-for-profit biotech organization that improves the lives of children with life-threatening rare diseases. Their digital platform aims to methodically leverage all layers of intelligence to efficiently develop treatments and drive real-life improvements for these children and their families. And their sustainability-focused business model increases both business and social impacts.

As we can see, there is an important difference between the digitalization of the existing business model and a digital transformation toward a new business model. While process automation, reimagination, and operating model change can often be done locally, such as in an engineering department, a business model transformation cuts across divisions and business functions. It requires new leadership and backing from the board(s) and then can be a highly effective lever for systematically driving digital transformation in a coherent way.

Business model transformation is also a viable means to reaching resilience. A business model is the distinctive logic of how to create value in the back end, deliver value in the front end to customers and other stakeholders, and capture value via the monetization mechanics for the organization. As illustrated in Figure 2, we can classify business models along two dimensions, which lead to four types: product, project, platform, and solution. Within the same industry sector, the business model types with higher inclusiveness have been better off because, on average, they showed higher resilience during the pandemic.

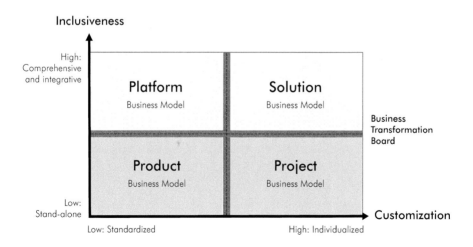

**Figure 2.** Transforming business models to build resilience.

Increasing inclusiveness can be achieved when the comprehensiveness of the offering and/or the stickiness of the business transaction is enhanced via a platform or solution business models. This implies moving from standalone, often physical offerings with vastly independent transactions, to comprehensive and integrated offerings with recurring transactions.

With higher inclusiveness levels, we have generally witnessed an increase in resilience (Linz, 2020). The higher the offering's breadth and depth, the bigger the ecosystem around its customers, and the more premium services are integrated (e.g., free-of-charge shipping, unique content), the less reasons exist to change vendors. Furthermore, subscription-based monetization models increase the probability that the customer will continue the relationship with the same vendor and often leads to a chain of transactions.

Certain sectors illustrate how leaders can foster inclusiveness in their business model to positively influence their firm's resilience:

- In financial services, retail banking is shrinking as demonstrated by Deutsche Bank closing every fifth outlet in their home market. In contrast, banking-as-a-service platforms, such as Railsbank or Solarisbank, have proved their resilience. Also, family offices, which provide holistic solutions, demonstrate resilience in times of capital market volatility.
- In manufacturing, traditional producers face downward pressure on demand, production, and supply chains. At the same time, digitalization of production and logistics accelerates with more connectivity, advanced analytics, automation, and advanced-manufacturing technologies. Companies that provide value-added services on their platforms could rely on recurring revenue streams, such as Siemens or Microsoft Azure or AWS, with their resilient Internet of Things (IoT) platform models.
- In professional services, consulting companies have shown that they can build on their long-standing customer relationships, even in a crisis, and now can blend remote and on-site delivery seamlessly. Some consulting firms even productized their project knowledge, built up intellectual property, and shifted into platform business models such as Infosys; hence proving business model transformation is an effective lever for digital transformation.

As we can see, customization does not increase resilience per se but provides important flavors of additional resilience. Increasing customization means moving from standardized, packaged, and automated offerings to individualized offerings that are cocreated by the company and customer. The resulting tighter provider–customer bond and the accumulation of domain-specific knowledge bolsters resilience in a time of crisis.

With regard to their business model, companies need to cultivate an openness toward a better future, no matter how much they have already invested in going down a specific path. When thinking about flexibility, it should not be defensive but offensive.

Smart leaders make sure that 20% to 30% of their transformation initiatives are focused on new business models and ideally drive new digital-native revenue streams. In a disrupted world, they invest in strategic resilience and focus on inclusive—comprehensive and sticky business models—such as platforms and solutions.

## Opportunity 4: Establish New Digital Operating Models for Sensing Organizations

In the age of extreme uncertainty, leaders often recognize that their organizations are working in operating models of the past, which are ill-suited to this highly uncertain environment. On the other hand, they know what they need: agility, flexibility, and collaboration across the organization. In other words, the approach used in a crisis mode can serve as a starting point: build a structure, a small group of trusted managers who have the judgment and internal credibility; have a broad network across the organization; and who can count on top-level support when big stakes are required. After crises, this temporary structure is usually dismantled again because the effort is very high, resources are overstretched, and employees would burn out. In the age of extreme uncertainty, however, we need agility, flexibility, and collaboration, not just temporarily, but on a continuous basis.

This means throwing out the playbook. In the 1990s, management theorist Steve Haeckel introduced to the business world a concept borrowed from cell biology: *sensing-responding-adapting* (Haeckel, 1999). The idea behind it was simple: the advent of information technology had enabled companies to be more flexible and responsive to changing customer needs and market conditions, leading to a new way of developing strategy. Thirty years later, technology has matured enough to make this concept a reality. Today, winners are creating new operating models that allow them not only to respond quickly to unpredictable conditions, but also to proactively shape the future of their businesses.

To turn this concept into reality, executives need to create a *digital nerve center* to holistically monitor both short-term crisis responses and strategic redesigns to ensure long-term survival. This allows the organization to move from deterministic prior year plans + 10% revenue, carefully prepared status reports that are out of date before they reach the board meeting, and processes too rigid for a timely response towards real-time or at least up-to-date information. Expanding information and awareness capabilities across the enterprise leads to greater enterprise resilience. It enables decision makers to fully understand the impact of decisions on the entire enterprise.

Technically, a digital nerve center requires a move away from isolated, tribal knowledge-based planning and decision-making, which is typically based on incomplete, fragmented, and siloed data scattered across multiple systems, often based on static tables and charts. Instead, it builds on a centralized, semantically correct data model that connects all key functions with real-time market and business data. It uses artificial intelligence (AI) to automate repetitive tasks, optimize processes, and generate insights that provide end-to-end visibility into the impact of decisions, enabling continuous learning and network effects. It also includes a digital monitoring and early warning system to better understand which events might trigger your business and integrates real-time knowledge, including leading indicators of market, demand, and supply.

Digital nerve centers recognize that, in a highly uncertain environment, genius comes from a collection of many people with different experiences and perspectives, which we like to call *crowds* and *ecosystems*. They enable seamless collaboration across functions and geographies and help create an organizational context for people to cocreate the future. Today, power lies more outside than inside the organization. It is less about the leader and more about the ship, with its blurring boundaries between inside and outside.

Consequently, such an "intelligent" organization can be seen as an amorphous entity that changes its structure over time to reflect the impulses in its environment and continuously evolves toward new, dynamic, and uncertain

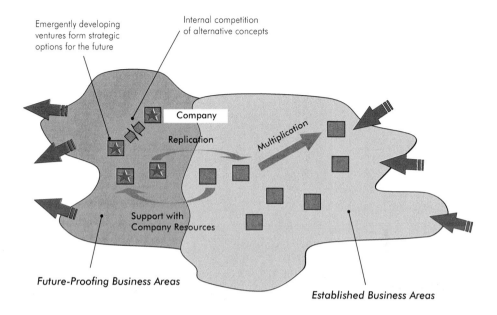

**Figure 3.** Organizational learning at the edges and building future options.

markets to develop innovative business areas (Figure 3). Its core competence is learning at the periphery of the organization. Given sufficient entrepreneurial capacity for strategic options, the margins can be interpreted as a transitional stage to new markets, where organizational vanguards explore and exploit new business opportunities. Their development is enhanced by the provision of group skills and resources. Conversely, the group also benefits by building new competency bases that are first acquired by these vanguards and then successively replicated and possibly multiplied as best practices throughout the organization.

## Conclusion: A Journey Strengthening Resilience

Life and business is a journey, not an event. Leadership in extremely uncertain environments requires a long-term perspective, a focus on purpose, a willingness to innovate and transform, and a constant focus on fast learning to seize the opportunity in the contradiction. Building teams that can weather uncertainty and change requires creating systems for support and dialogue. This is in stark contrast to toughness, but strengthens resilience.

# References

Chamorro-Premuzic, T., Lusk, D. (2017). The dark side of resilience. *Sloan Management Review*, August 16.

Corporate Leaders. (2019). Digital transformation survey: Creating products and services in a digital world. https://www.ptc.com/-/media/Files/PDFs/PLM/Digital_Transformation_Survey_Final_WEB_Single_Amend.pdf?la=en&hash=EC8F21EE8E86D3CED08C0BF1990F2FCD

Epstein, D. (2019). *Range: Why generalists triumph in a specialized world.* Riverhead Books.

EPU. (2022, March 21). *Economic policy uncertainty index.* https://www.policyuncertainty.com/

Haeckel, S.H. (1999). *Adaptive enterprise: Creating and leading sense-and-respond organizations.* Harvard Business School Press.

International Institute for Applied Systems Analyses (2020, August 27). (TWI2050) Report: The digital revolution and sustainable development: Opportunities and challenges. https://previous.iiasa.ac.at/web/home/research/twi/Report2019.html

Linz, C. (2019). *New leadership. Thriving in the Intelligent Age.* Global Peter Drucker Forum. https://www.druckerforum.org/blog/newleadership-thriving-in-the-intelligent-age-by-dr-carsten-linz/

Linz, C. (2000). *Group as a founding company: Revolutionary innovation management in accelerated markets* (pp. 109–118). Springer Gabler.

Linz, C. (2020, Nov. 9). *How to transform your business model for a post-COVID future.* World Economic Forum. https://www.weforum.org/agenda/2020/11/transform-business-model-post-covid-future/

Linz, C., Mueller-Stewens, G., Zimmermann, A. (2021). *Radical business model transformation: How leading organizations have successfully adapted to disruption* (2nd ed.). Kogan Page.

Linz, C. (2022). *Leading into a sustainable future when there are no easy answers, before this decade is Out.* COP26 Whitepaper Preview Edition. future/io

Pierce J. R., Aguinis H. (2013). The too-much-of-a-good-thing effect in management. *Journal of Management.* 39(2), 313–338.

Roddewig, M. (2012). Flink wie Windhunde, zäh wie Leder, hart wie Kruppstahl. Deutsche Welle, Themen. https://p.dw.com/p/16hN5

Sinek, S. (2020). *Infinite game.* Portfolio Penguin.

Toussaint, K. (2022, May 3). From automated trains to vaccine production, Siemens is changing the world with digitization. *Fast Company*.

Williamson, O. E. (1999). Strategy as option on the future. *Sloan Management Review*, Spring, 117–126.

## About the Author

**Carsten Linz** is CEO and founder of Bluegain, a company which supports executives in transforming established companies at the intersection of digital, business model, and sustainability shift. During his almost 20 years in executive roles focused on software, data, and digitally fuelled growth, he has built several €100 million businesses and led company-wide transformation programs affecting more than 60,000 employees. Linz's most recent roles include Group Digital Officer at BASF, Business Development Officer at SAP, and Global Head of the Center for Digital Leadership. He has represented on various boards including the o9 Executive Council, Social Impact, and chairs Shareability's Technology & Innovation Committee. He is a member of the World Economic Forum's Expert Network on Digital Economy and New Leadership and of the investment committee of European's largest seed capital fund. He teaches on executive programs and acts as adviser to Executive and Supervisory Boards and CxOs around the world. He is the author of *Radical Business Model Transformation: Gaining the Competitive Edge in a Disruptive World* (Kogan-Page, 2017), which is considered a standard reference in business model and digital transformation literature.

# Conscious Resilience: A Framework for Building Resilient Organizations

HABEEB MAHABOOB, PADMINI RAMAMURTHY, AND HULIGESHWARI DEVI

16

# The Case for Organizational Resilience

Only in minds with fertile imagination there exists a business world where nothing breaks down, no calamity occurs, or no unforeseen situations happen. The recent COVID-19 pandemic, global financial crisis, wars, and extreme weather conditions have constantly reminded us of the stark realities that businesses and organizations must face. While an organization can plan for a *rainy day*, it is humanly impossible to predict and plan for all possibilities that could disrupt normalcy. Given this, the next best thing to do is to make an organization tolerant, robust, and adaptable—in short, make it a resilient organization.

## Defining Organizational Resilience

There is an old Japanese adage that states: "The bamboo that bends is stronger than the oak that resists." Our idea of organizational resilience is built on this thought. A resilient organization must be defined around not just building strong fences and defenses, but also on building inherent flexibility and adaptability to respond to unforeseen situations. Organizational resilience is a capability and also definable around the outcomes that come from being resilient.

Resilience is the inherent ability of an organization to thrive amid unexpected events impacting the organization. Organizational resilience is the ability of an organization to not only recover from crisis or convert threats to opportunities but to thrive by reaching a better point of stability than before.

Resilience is a complex function of:
- Quantum of advantage: Positive or negative change in an organization's outcomes during or post an event
- Stability: How many disruptions can continue to occur without threatening the normal course of work
- Scope/span: How many/much of its service/work can be recovered from failure or can be adapted to new requirements
- Time: How fast an organization can recover from a failure, or how fast an organization can adapt to a change

### Framework for Organizational Resilience

The Conscious Resilience framework (Figure 1) is a transformation framework for building organizational resilience. Our point of view is that resilience or the act of becoming resilient is an acquired capability that is built over a period of time. A resilient organization builds a set of practices that support resilience and develop a culture that catalyzes and sustains it. In our view, mature organizations consciously make choices that enhance resilience, hence the term Conscious Resilience.

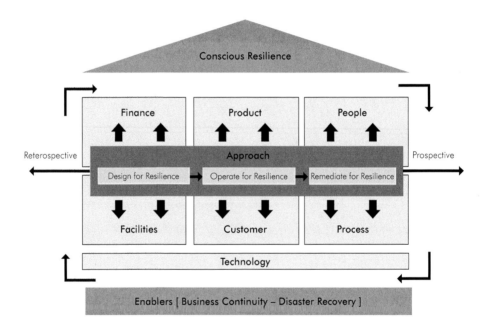

**Figure 1**. Framework for conscious resilience.

The framework's core ethos is an iterative approach of design–operate–remediate for building a resilient organization across seven different domains or dimensions, namely finance, facilities, product, process, people, customer, and technology. The enablers for building resilient organizations are practices of business continuity and disaster recovery.

## Finance Domain

Financials drive organizational health and decision-making. Processes, such as accounts receivable, cash flow management, profit and loss management, and cash reserve management, to cite a few, can be grouped under the finance domain. Finance strategy should have a long- and near-term focus. When organizations stay vigilant and prepared, they can tide through unforeseen situations. A global manufacturer suffered extensively when its prime product was restricted to only select usage due to countrywide safety restrictions. The organization was saved owing to its financial resilience practices. The organization had been proactively saving for the unknowns. Healthy cash reserves enabled the organization to continue business, thereby retaining existing talent. The stable environment motivated employees to contribute. The organization was quick to think on its feet and refocused on another brand in their portfolio.

## Facilities Domain

All physical and virtual aspects, such as buildings, manufacturing facilities, transportation, warehouses, cabling, power systems, cooling/heating facilities, and so forth of an organization's work setup can be termed facilities domain. Resilient organizations make balanced decisions on facility locations to avoid a concentration of similar types of work. In addition, they also design, build, and test plans and procedures if some of the facilities are rendered unavailable. Here is an example of the complexities involved in planning resilient facilities. For one of the customers for whom a leading IT service provider delivered services from one of the sites, all employees were working from home due to the COVID-19 pandemic. So, the office facilities were shut down, but now individual employees' homes had been turned into mini home offices to enable service delivery and business continuity. Amid this situation, the site was hit by a typhoon; as a result, all internet and power facilities shut down. This rendered all employees of this site unreachable even though they were in their home offices. It was only because the company had planned for resilience at the core of service delivery, alternate home offices at a different site were made available. Technical call routing and load balancing with other site home offices ensured service availability. With this approach, the pandemic and typhoon crises could be easily managed.

## Product Domain

Products built by an organization, a supply chain supporting them, and the services offered form the product domain. Resilient organizations choose their portfolio of products carefully to ensure minimal impact due to unforeseen events. These events may relate to sudden changes in customer needs, supply chain disruptions, and government and regulatory changes. Product diversification and market system resilience are aspects that help organizations remain sustainable and flourish. One of the electronics companies added a range of water heaters to their existing air cooler products. This helped the organization build a resilient product portfolio. Organizations should review their product portfolio to identify concentrations, the impact of unforeseen events, and take action to reduce product portfolio risks.

## Process Domain

All of the methods, practices, policies, and steps to accomplish certain tasks can be grouped under the process domain. Processes bring structure and shape to the work; they also provide predictability to achieve intended outcomes. Hence, for building resilience, a focus on process is critical. However, overinvestment in a process-centric view of work makes an organization rigid. The more modular, decentralized, and agile a process, the more likely it is to adapt to changes or handle failures. Conscious resilience is all about creating this agility in processes. This agility could be brought in through several ways, such as taking a localized approach to creating processes, standardizing only essential parts, simplification of processes, and automating processes where it makes sense. Conscious resilient organizations provide flexibility to their teams in adopting practices around a specific guideline, without a hard focus on process compliance alone. While creating practices, the focus should be to unearth and plan for the numerous ways in which processes can fail and the alternatives to achieving intended outcomes.

## People Domain

Organizational structure, staffing plans, and practices that have touchpoints with people (e.g., recruiting) can be grouped under the people domain. People are the most critical part of any organization's business; hence, building organizational resilience must start from here. Resilient organizations consciously inculcate policies and practices that support resilience in a holistic manner, both at the individual employee and macro-organizational levels. Succession planning with a view on business continuity, key staff identification, and multiskilling are all good practices that resilient organizations follow. One of the large IT providers made a policy during the COVID-19 pandemic to ensure leadership does not collectively attend in-person meetings at the same time. Organizations should systematically identify people skill concentrations and take active measures to reduce risk.

## Customer Domain

Customer portfolio management is at the core of this domain. Qualification of customers prior to customer acquisition can prevent impacts due to unforeseen events to customers' businesses. Diversification of the customer base across industries and geographies helps avoid the concentration of customers and minimizes risk. Organizations are more resilient when they adopt a cocreation mindset in partnership with the customer. It is also essential to plan for resilience with the customer's competition in mind. One of the global IT firms took a conscious decision to limit the share of revenue from an individual customer to less than 20% of the total. Organizations must plan their portfolio of customers, keeping these practices in mind.

## Technology Domain

Irrespective of the industry or domain, technology resilience is critical for organizations. Cyberattacks, capacity challenges, legacy infrastructure, poor technical architecture, and unplanned deployments are some of the causes of technology failure. In recent times, we have seen large organizations encounter major outages due to one or more of the above reasons. Resilient organizations have a thorough understanding of how technology fails and have strategies to proactively address it. A cohesive security strategy, multicloud adoption strategy, proactive assessment of scalability requirements, chaos engineering practices, and structured deployments are some of the best practices for resilient organizations. A subscription streaming service and production company designed chaos engineering tools to test system stability by enforcing failures via the pseudo random termination of instances and services within their architecture. Organizations should have a strategy that identifies points of failures and proactively build for resilience. Table 1 provides a summary of the framework.

Table 1. Summary of the Framework

| | Design | Operate | Remediate |
|---|---|---|---|
| **Finance** | Financial policies to ensure management of financial risks (e.g., cash flow decisions, overdraft, credit limit). | All operating decisions that have a financial impact should be reviewed from risk and resilience perspectives. | Identify past decisions, policies, or current practices that need to be rectified from a resilience perspective. |
| **People** | Modular agile operating model. | Key role identification and succession planning as a normal feature in day-to-day operations. | Review hiring practices, and job rotation policies from a resilience perspective. |
| **Process** | Structured, clear, precise, yet flexible (e.g., if automated processes die, alternative manual processes can be designed). | Build flexibility to structure and define processes from practices learned during recovery situations. | In retrospective, review all current processes from resilience and prospective views. |
| **Facilities** | Ensure facilities backup available or alternate means to continue services/work. | Test for recovery periodically, run disaster recovery (DR) tests/drills periodically. | Review all changes to facilities/new locations from the perspective of resilience. |
| **Customer** | Plan customer acquisition with resilience in mind. (e.g., no more than 20% of your total revenue from a single customer). | All customer delivery decisions to be reviewed from risk and resilience perspectives. | Review and remediate all current customer acquisition practices from a resilience perspective. |
| **Product** | Design portfolio of products/services with resilience in mind: diversify. | Review all product changes/upgrade decisions with a resilience perspective. | Remediate product decisions with a resilience perspective. |
| **Technology** | Design with identified nonfunctional requirements (NFRs); institutionalize chaos engineering practices to understand how technology enablers can fail. | Create the right service level objectives (SLOs) and service level indicators (SLIs).<br><br>Major incident management and communication practices. | Remediate all IT policies with a resilience perspective. |

### Culture of Conscious Resilience

We have identified a need for a culture that spans across all of the domains as a key enabler for organizational resilience. We define this as conscious resilience in our framework.

"Culture eats strategy for breakfast" is a well-known quote from Peter Drucker on the importance of culture over strategy. For resilient organizations, what matters is not just the approach taken across the various domains, but also the culture that sustains and grows it. Based on our experience, we believe there are a few features that need to be consciously embedded in resilient organizations:

- **A culture of encouraging objective questioning toward risk identification and prevention:** Mature organizations have mechanisms that allow objective questioning at all levels to review risks and escalate findings up to the board. Clearly defined policies to manage risks are available.

- **A culture of blamelessness:** For organizations to be objectively able to handle failures/changes, it is important to see failures/changes as they are without associating emotions. It is necessary to disassociate blaming, especially if they vilify individuals. Management and leadership play a large role in inculcating this culture. By simply displaying the right attitude toward failures or by diverting the attention of teams toward problem-solving during a failure, blamelessness as a cultural attribute can be stressed.

- **A practice of celebrating failures:** By this, we don't mean that all failed programs must be rewarded. The underlying message is that only when organizations know what failure is or what change means, will they know how to build resilience. Hence, organizations must reward practices that unearth potential failures and processes that enable faster adaptation to changes. Additionally, programs must be based on the principle of fail fast and move forward.

- **Ingrained learning methods from failures:** A structured approach to learning post facto must be highly encouraged. Leaders and managers participating in such post facto learning exercises provide a clear message to staff and ingrain a culture of learning from failures.

## The Rear and Forward Views

The retrospective (rear) and prospective (forward) views that guide organizations to make decisions with resilience form the concluding part of our framework. Conscious resilience needs organizations to develop a deep understanding of issues they have faced in the past as well as potential issues and opportunities they may face in future, while designing and operating for resilience. Traditional approaches used for continuity planning, such as business impact analysis, risk assessment, and development of resilience strategies, can be adopted to develop resilience strategies. However, on many occasions, typical human biases prevent us from developing views about the future. Intense listening at the edges by senior management and the use of schedule and event-based activities to assess resilience will ensure that an organization's resilience plans are robust.

## Business Continuity and Disaster Recovery

While resilience is a higher-order imperative for organizations, setting up the basic foundational elements of business continuity and disaster recovery continue to be a key enabler. Organizations need to significantly think through how they react to and recover from unforeseen events. Systematic application of techniques, such as business impact analysis, risk strategy, and devising a thought-through disaster recovery and business continuity plan, must be parts of the overall resilience agenda.

## Implementation and Maturity Model for Organizational Resilience

Our experience suggests that organizations need to intentionally build resilience into everything they do. Mature organizations take a holistic view of resilience and build resilience into how they design and operate every part of their business. Our maturity model spans across the three dimensions of design, operate, and remediate. At the adaptive state—a nirvana state for organizational resilience—organizations benefit from unforeseen circumstances. This happens by the virtue of focus on resilience in design decisions, reduced resilience debt, and the organizational mindset focused on failure prevention and business growth. Reaching this stage requires structured implementation of organizational resilience practices at all levels, as depicted in Figure 2.

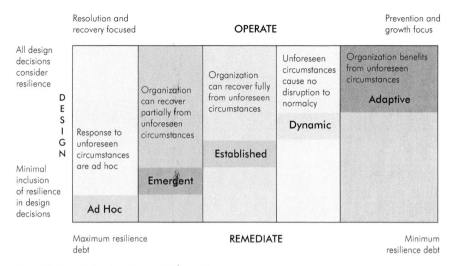

Figure 2. Organizational resilience maturity model.

## Call to Action

Given that businesses today must live through turbulent and unforeseen situations, it is imperative for all organizations to build organizational resilience in a structured manner. A good starting point is to build resilience into all of the people aspects from the beginning, while scaling resilience practices across all other domains. A comprehensive assessment based on our conscious resilience framework will help organizations unearth opportunities to build and improve resilience.

## About the Authors

**Habeeb Mahaboob** is Managing Partner at Tech Mahindra's consulting division, Business Excellence, Inc. (BE) based in Chicago, Illinois, USA.

**Padmini Ramamurthy** is a Principal Consultant specializing in Technology Resilience at Business Excellence, Inc. (BE) based in Bangalore, India.

**Huligeshwari Devi** is a Principal Consultant specializing in Process Resilience at Business Excellence, Inc., (BE) based in Lansing, Michigan, USA.

Business Excellence, Inc. is the consulting division of Tech Mahindra. It helps clients achieve their business objectives in the Digital Age. Tech Mahindra is one of the fastest growing brands among the top 15 IT service providers globally and represents the connected world, offering innovative, customer centric information technology experiences.

# The Path to Resilience: What It Takes to Thrive in the Accelerated Future

TERENCE MAURI

# 17

In the last two years everything has changed. People changed. The office changed. Technology changed. Leadership changed. And the way we think about resilience changed. Welcome to the big jolt—an age of risk and opportunity marked by accelerating and overlapping waves of disruptions, from red-hot inflation and democratic backlashes to the war in Ukraine and a global pandemic. Leaders around the world, in every industry, must now confront challenges both practical and existential. Some have failed. Many have simply survived. I believe that a change in perspective is worth at least 80 IQ points, because your current perceptions are grounded in your past assumptions. This starts with reframing and reimagining what resilience means for your work, workplace, and workforce. Re-perception—the ability to see, hear, or become aware of something new in existing information and notice the blind spots we don't see—is at the heart of making resilience a leader's North Star, alongside trust, growth, and talent. To help leaders do so, it is worth asking several questions: What is resilience and how do you sustain it in the long term? What are the mindset shifts, assumptions, and risks for this journey? And what do you say no to or unlearn to become 10 times more resilient at performing for today while transforming for tomorrow?

Resilience is a form of future readiness and an accelerant for transformation and growth. At its core, resilience is a company's capacity to anticipate, absorb, and respond to the forces of disruption. Change used to happen like a breeze. Now it feels like a category-five typhoon. Business, supply chain, and workforce disruptions are accelerating, and business models and leadership models are decaying faster than ever before from the blurring of industry lines, economic, and geopolitical turbulence, new platforms and shrinking product life spans, company life spans (50% of Standard & Poor's [S&P] 500 companies will not exist in 10 years at current churn rates), and even job life spans (1 billion people will need reskilling by 2025 according to the World Economic Forum [WEF]). With over US$41 trillion of enterprise value at risk and 93% of leaders expecting significant industry disruption over the next five years, resilience has become a leader's top call-to-action challenge. The world is more turbulent, less predictable, more complex, less simple, more infinite, and less knowable. It doesn't help that leaders' brains are hardwired to dislike uncertainty so they always find ways to avoid it.

General Electric (GE). Intel. Barnes & Noble. Business models are failing as fast as yogurt in the fridge, and competitive advantage has been fading faster than at any time in recent history. Just look at the floundering fortunes of indoor cycling upstart Peloton (its share price is down nearly 80% in the last 12 months). Now, the half-life of a company has shrunken to one year or less, and resilience is no longer a nice-to-have; yet, research at Hack Future Lab shows a huge gap between rhetoric and reality when it comes to building a resilient company with 82% of leaders saying resilience is important, but only one-half that number says it's a strength. Top-performing enterprises know that resilience is both a differentiating factor and a must have to learn, grow, and thrive in the present and the future.

Here are the qualities of resilient enterprises:

- Four times more energized and optimistic about the future
- Three and a half times more likely to be prochange leaders
- Have three times more capacity to turn a crisis into a growth opportunity
- Two and a half times better equipped at reframing failure as a platform for learning and experimenting.
- Twice more likely to have an iterative growth mindset versus a bureaucratic fixed mindset

The Finnish have a word called *sisu*, which means courage, grit, and resilience in the face of extreme adversity. When navigating the future, it is clear that fear and uncertainty still dominate the leadership narrative, and that elevating resilience across the enterprise is a blind spot for most leaders. Consider the Great Resignation (record levels of employees quitting their jobs), the Big Quit, and the Great Reassessment (two-thirds of employees rethinking their purpose at work). Add to that the Turnover Tsunami, the Attrition Supercycle, the Hybrid Paradox (what's your workforce's hybrid strategy?), and the Race to Reskill (the best ways to bake resilience into leadership and enterprise resilience are upskilling, reskilling, and cross-skilling). It's no wonder that, according to Hack Future Lab's Global Leader's Resilience Index, 78% of leaders report record levels of burnout, mental exhaustion, and anticipatory anxiety about the future. Anticipatory anxiety and resilience are like oil and water—a performance killer. So, what leadership actions and bold moves are needed to be resilient in the accelerated future when today is the slowest it will ever be?

When you think about it everything starts as an act of imagination, but to sustain vitality for the long-term leaders must harness resilience. Resilience is the human force that can help leaders bounce back and spring forward from setbacks and turn uncertainty into action. To define the path to resilience for leaders, Hack Future Lab embarked on a research initiative to understand how a select few companies have flourished, transforming their businesses and illuminating the way forward for others, despite what United Nations Secretary General Antonio Guterres calls a code red for leadership as we confront the triple crises of climate emergency, conflict, and the COVID-19 pandemic. The pandemic put leaders under acute levels of cognitive and emotional stress and highlighted who is ready for the many changes the future will bring—and who is not. In times of crisis, resilience is a multiplier of future readiness, such as the capacity to explore early-to-exploit know-how sooner, and requires the curiosity to learn and the courage to unlearn. Learning helps leaders evolve, and unlearning helps leaders keep up as the world evolves. The research identified three imperatives, which we believe separate resilient, sustainable companies from the pack when a sudden and unfavorable change in the operating environment occurs.

## Imperative One: Attention is the New Oil

Data isn't the new oil. Attention is the new oil. Attention to context setting, pace setting, and direction setting. Attention to learning and unlearning. Attention to shaping a bold future and learning to be deliberately resilient in a world, *The Economist* calls "predictability unpredictable." The problem is that it is difficult to be resilient when you're burned out, with 78% of leaders saying they "struggle to focus on what matters" and 53% saying they "spend too much energy on shallow work (low value, low impact) at the expense of deep work" (high value, high impact). Leaders are tired. Zoom fatigue. Meeting fatigue. Collaboration fatigue. Solution fatigue. Brain fog. The Nobel laureate Herbert A. Simon said: "Too much information leads to a poverty of attention." Leaders pay a price every time attention is hijacked by a pointless meeting or we schedule back-to-back Zoom calls with no free time during the day for reflecting and refueling.

Leaders should not waste the biggest reframing moment of their careers. So, what can be done differently today to help your enterprise achieve the highest return on attention, which is crucial for a bold and resilient future?

1. **Focus on velocity, not speed.**

   The reason is simple. Speed is the time rate at which you're moving along a path, whereas velocity is the rate and direction you're heading in. Speed without aligned direction can lead to inertia or focus drift and waste precious time and resources.

2. **Fight complexity with simplicity.**

   When you run into a problem you can't solve, don't make it smaller—make it bigger. Today's challenges can't be solved with yesterday's thinking. Thinking small and being an incrementalist deplete your ambition and energy. You'll ignite purpose and spark new ideas and fresh perspectives when you embrace the urgency and scale of your biggest challenges.

3. **Have meeting-free days.**

   It sounds obvious, but you're having too many meetings! Hack Future Lab's research highlights that since the pandemic, the number of back-to-back meetings has doubled and are often scheduled with no breaks in between. Too many wasteful meetings lead to a higher cognitive and leadership toll. Having a meeting-free day increases autonomy, engagement, focus, and resilience by three times.

4. **Have a "no" strategy.**

   Hack Future Lab's research highlights that 83% of leaders are drowning in too many priorities and over commitments. This erodes attention and doubles the risk of shallow work versus deep work. A "no" strategy is one of the best forms of optimization and a powerful way to protect attention. It's a clarifier, a simplifier, and a multiplier of ROI. Not return on investment. Return on *Intelligence*.

Without deliberate attention to your inner world (blind spots, reflection, learning) and outer world (people, risks, growth), it's difficult to stay ahead of change and be resilient. Hack Future Lab's research shows that leaders with heightened levels of inner attention and outer attention are significantly better at embracing humility to their blind spots and biases, as well as spotting risks before they become emergencies and seizing new paths to growth. Leading a future that is bold and resilient is not about time—it's about thoughtful attention to yourself, others, and the world around you.

## Imperative Two: Trust is Your Workforce and Resilience Multiplier

Money is the currency of transactions, and trust is the currency of resilience. Trust is a shortcut to resilience and it's the foundation of every leadership action, relationship, and decision. It's time to rethink trust: Customer. Employee. Digital. Financial. Ethical. Yet, around the world, we see truth decay and record levels of distrust across businesses, governments, and the media. According to Hack Future Lab, 10 out of 15 industry sectors have reported a decline in trust over the last three years and there are plenty of examples of major trust breaches, from the devastating Boeing Max 737 crashes to McKinsey's opioid settlement, and the once high-flying payment processor Wirecard crashing into insolvency after admitting that €1.9 billion in cash was missing and that large parts of the business had been misrepresented. At no time has trust been more tested or more valued by customers, leaders, and one another.

As we transition to remote and hybrid work models, humans, machines, workforce ecosystems, and talent marketplaces, there are fear and excitement. In the short term these will come from the unknown business fallout of a pandemic and, in the medium term, from the continued impact and opportunities of artificial intelligence (AI), robots, and automation. Hack Future Lab's research shows that 83% of leaders see trust playing a far greater role in sustaining a resilient workforce in a post-COVID-19 world. Resilient enterprises, such as games developer Roblox and e-commerce leader, Block (formerly Square), report that high-trust employees are:

- Three times more likely to act as an early warning system for leaders when companies are operating at the edge of ethics as they are more likely to speak up and call out issues.
- Two and a half times as likely as distrusted employees to be excited about the prospect of reskilling and three times more likely to be satisfied with the company, with no plans to leave.
- Twice as likely to say their enterprise is transparent about which jobs will change, and rank uncertainty last in reasons for feeling burned out.

Hack Future Lab's research shows that future-ready leaders embrace trust as an accelerator of resilience and emphasize three things: truth, transparency, and trust, placing ethical drivers at the heart of their leadership style. Leaders who unlock trust have decided to pivot from command-and-control leadership to care and cocreation, from control to freedom and autonomy, and from talent hoarding to talent creation and enablement. Not only that, they are three times more energizing to work for and better equipped at reframing failure as a platform for learning and experimenting.

Trust and resilience are inseparable and vital to taking trust leaps into the future, from navigating uncertainty and reducing risk to adopting new frameworks and agile ways of working. Without trust, relationships break down, enterprises stop working, and leaders fail. In an age with record levels of distrust brought on by social tension, economic nationalism, and technological revolution, it's time for leaders to reassess how to bake trust into the DNA, strategy, and day-to-day operations of their business. This will sustain trust across the whole stakeholder mix, from employees, to customers, suppliers, investors, analysts, and the media. Now is not the time to adopt a wait-and-see strategy. As beacons of trust, leaders need a more expansive view of their mandate and should make trust a priority across competence and consistency (how you do things) and integrity and empathy (why you do things). Put trust at the forefront of your leadership, strategy, and purpose and it will become a vital source of resilience and future preparedness for your enterprise.

## Imperative Three: Lead From the Future

Albert Einstein said: "You can't use an old map to explore a new world." New contexts demand new mindsets and leadership behaviors that can adapt at the pace of the external environment. A great starting point to being resilient is to practice reframing and reimagining. Are you writing the success headlines for the future, today? What will be your proudest moments and boldest milestones? And what changes do you need to make now to get started? In an operating environment that is high certainty, stable, and predictable, the ratio of assumptions to knowledge is low enough to repeat the same strategy and leadership behaviors over a long time line. Today is different. Network effects, speed of scale, speed of change, speed of innovation, and high asset productivity mean that competitive lines are being redrawn three times faster than 10 years ago. Paypal, for example, has a market cap two and a half times bigger than 151-year-old Goldman Sachs and has registered 1,500 patents in the last five years (26 times more than Goldman Sachs).

One of the clearest signs of resilience is rethinking your assumptions and updating your opinions to avoid strategy, transformation, or culture drift. When the ratio of assumptions to knowledge is high and the operating environment is volatile, the best way of staying relevant is to lead from the future (not the past). Most leaders are trapped in a present-forward strategy, whereby they simply extend their existing mental models, ideas, and assumptions about the world to the future. Companies that decide to lead from the future align on a shared view of the future and work backward from that point. Research at Hack Future Lab analyzed 100 companies that are leading from the future across different sectors, including Moderna reimagining pharmaceuticals using mRNA—the software of life; Beyond Meat reimagining food technology for a healthy and ecologically friendly future; and Klarna the buy now, pay later (BNPL) decacorn, disrupting the US$8 trillion card payment market to identify what made them future prepared and resilient.

Lead from the future accelerators include:
- A strong shared view of the future
- Urgency to act
- Digitally obsessed
- Inclusivity at scale
- Always-learning workforce
- Treat culture like a product, e.g., iterative and curiosity led
- Building talent marketplaces and workforce ecosystems

Pfizer is known for its nine-month race to make the impossible possible by creating the first COVID-19 vaccine in the world. What you may not know is that Pfizer Chairman and CEO Dr. Albert Bourla is on a mission to harness uncertainty as a tailwind to lead from the future by activating lightspeed behaviors across the 79,000-person enterprise (act at the speed of science, crush bureaucracy, believe in the purpose, and trust one another) and bringing values to life every day (courage, equity, excellence, and joy at work). Bourla, a provocateur of bold action, knows that to change the game you must make game-changing moves. The result is resilience on the human scale in the forms of:

- Reskilling and upskilling all employees with future-fit skills by 2025.
- Scaling cultures of resilience based on high-risk tolerance for experimentation.
- Engaging employees by aligning opportunities to their own sense of purpose.
- Improving agility (enterprise agility, talent agility, hiring agility, and workforce agility) to maintain business continuity.

- Democratizing career development and increasing workforce visibility.
- Unlearn the "always done it this way," e.g., letting go of obsolete behaviors.

A key takeaway is that, after money, the number one reason employees leave their jobs is a lack of internal growth opportunities. It turns out that businesses that lead from the future build cultures of resilience around moving talent to where the value is at speed and further accelerate the transformation toward a more agile, resilient, and empowered enterprise.

The path to resilience is not easy and requires courage of heart and boldness of ideas. The fear of losing in the near term is a clear and present danger, but the threat of losing relevance looms even larger. Leaders always overestimate the risk of trying something new and underestimate the risk of standing still. That's why becoming a resilient enterprise is non negotiable, but it takes intention and grit to drive it. The Japanese word *Henka* (変化) means everlasting change and transcendence and takes its inspiration from nature. It's turning lead into gold, a caterpillar into a butterfly, or oil into water. To win in the accelerated future, leaders should embrace *Henka* as a catalyst for leading and embracing perpetual resilience. If there's a final call to action that I can offer every leader: make this the year you do something bold because leadership is never finished. Transformation is never finished. Culture is never finished. Learning is never finished. Make it the year you take smart risks, fight complexity with simplicity, adopt new agile ways of leading and working, and say goodbye to the status quo. Make it the year of resilience, not fear.

## About the Author

**Terence Mauri** has been described as "an influential and outspoken thinker on the future of leadership" by Thinkers50. He is the founder of a global management think tank, Hack Future Lab, an Entrepreneur-Mentor-in-Residence at MIT, and an adjunct professor at IE Business School, where he lectures in the Advanced Management Program. His latest book is *The 3D Leader: Take Your Leadership to the Next Dimension* (FT Publishing International, 2020).

# Transforming for Resilience

MARTIN REEVES

**18**

During the COVID-19 crisis, resilience rose to the top of the strategic agenda, as many leaders indicated a desire to extract lessons to increase preparedness for future crises. As the economy recovered, the Ukraine war hit, disrupting energy and food supply chains and providing a second reason to focus on resilience.

Although less emphasized in stable periods, our research indicates that resilience creates significant value and does so well beyond times of crisis. Nearly two-thirds of long-run outperformers do better than their peers in response to shocks.

Crises often precipitate or accentuate the need to transform because of the immediate pressure on performance. Crisis-driven transformations often aim to ameliorate performance pressure by increasing cost and asset efficiency. But what is their impact on resilience and long-term performance? And how can companies transform for not only efficiency but also resilience?

To better understand the impact of large-scale change programs on building resilience, we applied an evidence-based approach to study over 1,200 corporate transformations over the last 25 years. The evidence indicates that roughly one-half of corporate transformations fail to improve resilience in response to future crises. Analyzing the same dataset also offers valuable insights into how some companies successfully transform for resilience.

**Measuring the Impact of a Resilient Transformation**

To study the success factors of a resilient transformation, we must first quantify the total value created by resilient companies in response to crises. Our past research has identified three stages post shock during which resilience creates value relative to peers:

- First, the immediate impact of a shock can be lower than peer's by better absorbing the shock.
- Second, higher recovery speeds by rapidly adapting to new circumstances.
- Finally, a greater recovery extent (12-month period following a shock) by reimagining their business to flourish in new circumstances.

Cumulatively, the relative performance (total shareholder return [TSR] benchmarked to industry median) across all three stages is the total value of resilience displayed in response to a crisis (Figure 1).

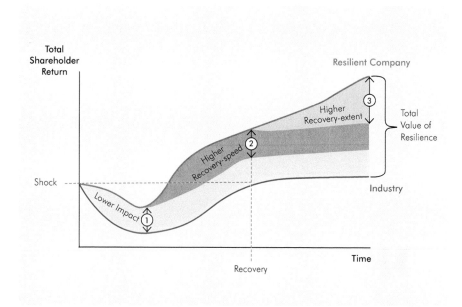

**Figure 1.** Total value of resilience realized across three stages: shock, recovery, and higher recovery-extent.

Source: BCG Henderson Institute Analysis

To measure the impact of change programs on resilience, we studied the difference in total resilience in response to industry shocks during the five-year period following a corporate transformation. While roughly one-half of transformations fail to improve resilience, a significant spread in outcomes exists. The top quartile of resilient transformations improved performance relative to industry by 25 percentage points (pp) in response to future crises, whereas the bottom quartile saw a decline of 20 pp.

What can we learn from the outperformers?

1. **Growth acceleration is the main driver of a resilient transformation.** Whereas large-scale change programs, especially crisis-induced ones, typically target cost reduction, differential growth contributes most of the incremental value created by resilient transformations. Transformations that accelerate growth improve performance relative to industry during each stage of future crises (+6 pp total impact on average), whereas transformations that only reduce costs see future resilience decline.

2. **Transformations that reduce debt and increase flexibility improve resilience.** Transformations that reduce debt loads improve the ability to cushion the immediate impact of a future shock. Furthermore, transformations that reduce fixed asset intensity boost adaptivity and recovery speed by shifting costs toward variable expenses. Growth transformations that do both increase the odds of improving resilience from one-half to nearly two-thirds and yield an average change in TSR performance relative to industry of +10 pp in response to future crises.

3. **Transformations are empirically less likely to build resilience when a crisis is no longer fresh.** If history is any guide, resilience now risks losing its spot on the corporate agenda as the performance of economies and companies recovers. Immediately following a crisis, transformations are 19% more likely to be growth oriented and 20% less likely to increase debt than those at least 12 months removed. However, our research shows that allowing resilience to fall off the change agenda would be a mistake. In today's dynamic business environment, resilience has benefits across the whole economic cycle.

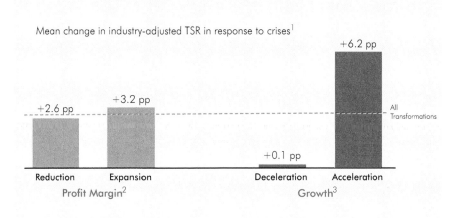

Mean change in industry-adjusted TSR in response to crises[1]

+6.2 pp

+3.2 pp

+2.6 pp

All Transformations

+0.1 pp

| Reduction | Expansion | | Deceleration | Acceleration |
| Profit Margin[2] | | | Growth[3] | |

1. Crisis quarter if peak decline in industry TSR exceeds 15 pp. Compares performance in response to industry shocks during 5-year periods preceding and following corporate transformation.
2. Margin expansion if 12-month EBIT margin after transformation end is greater than 12-month EBIT margin before transformation start; reduction otherwise.
3. Growth acceleration if trailing 12-month growth in full-year following end of transformation is greater than trailing 12-month growth at start of transformation; deceleration otherwise.

**Figure 2.** Growth drives resilient transformations.

Source: S&P Capital IQ; BCG Henderson Institute analysis

## Growth Drives Resilient Transformations

Our past research indicates that transformations often aim primarily at reducing costs. While this may improve performance in the short run, on average it does not lead to greater resilience in future crises. In contrast, transformations that accelerate growth, in aggregate, improve total resilience by +6 pp, whereas those that decelerate growth, on average, fail to improve resilience (Figure 2).

While growth transformations succeed in improving performance relative to industry during each of the three stages of future crises, nearly one-half of the improvement manifests in the extent of future recovery. In this third stage, after the recovery has taken hold, companies begin to reimagine their products and business models to thrive in the altered circumstances resulting from the shock. Growth-oriented transformations create significant advantage in this period by building the capability to spot and capitalize on new growth opportunities (Figure 3).

Mean change in industry-adjusted TSR in response to crises[1]

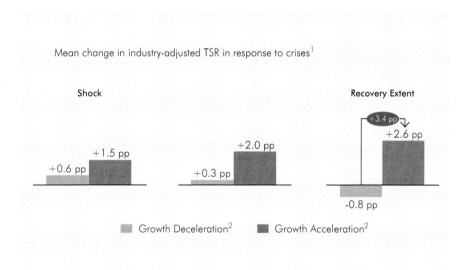

1. Crisis quarter if peak decline in industry TSR exceeds 15 pp. Compares performance in response to industry shocks during 5-year periods preceding and following corporate transformation.
2. Growth acceleration if trailing 12-month growth in full-year following end of transformation is greater than trailing 12-month growth at start of transformation; deceleration otherwise.

**Figure 3.** Growth transformation is an advantage especially for future recovery extent.

Source: S&P Capital IQ; BCG Henderson Institute analysis

For example, NVIDIA's 2015 corporate transformation restructured operations toward strategic-growth areas in deep learning, automated driving, and gaming. Following the transformation, NVIDIA doubled its growth rate over the next 12 months to 26%. With the semiconductor industry recovering to pre pandemic highs, NVIDIA once again shifted its strategic focus to identifying new growth drivers. In June 2020, the organization announced a partnership with Daimler AG unit Mercedes-Benz to build software-defined computing architecture for automated driving and in April 2021 unveiled the company's first data center graphics processing unit (GPU). Having previously performed in line with peers during post recovery periods, NVIDIA has thus far outperformed industry peers by +11 pp since the COVID-19 pandemic began in March 2020.

## Debt Reduction and Operational Flexibility Also Help

Transformations that reduce debt loads help companies cushion future shocks. Large-scale change efforts often require a significant financial commitment. In response, leaders may find it tempting—particularly in the low interest rate environment of the last decade—to fund change programs by increasing corporate debt. But doing so materially reduces resilience on average.

When a crisis hits, highly leveraged companies are more likely to struggle to sustain operations, as servicing debt is a higher fixed cost. It also limits the ability of corporations to tap into corporate debt markets during a future crisis—either to sustain operations or acquire distressed assets. Furthermore, investors often prefer the safety of corporations with lower debt levels amid the uncertainty of a crisis, compounding the problem.

Our research finds that growth transformations that reduce debt burdens (lower debt-to-enterprise value) increase performance relative to industry during future market dips by +2.5 pp on average, whereas those that increase debt burdens see a decline of -0.3 pp during the initial shock.

Consider *The New York Times* and its corporate transformation effort throughout the 2010s. After its debt burden briefly surpassed 200% of enterprise value during the global financial crisis, the company began rebalancing its portfolio of businesses and restructuring operations. After selling off several noncore business segments and entering a sale-leaseback agreement on its headquarters to free up capital, the organization began dramatically reducing debt and investing heavily in its paid digital subscription model. By the end of 2019, the organization announced it was debt-free and had increased digital revenue to US$800 million.

Without the higher burden of servicing debt, the organization was afforded a cushioning advantage, as advertising revenue contracted sharply at the beginning of the COVID-19 pandemic. Having struggled in past market shocks, *The New York Times* outperformed industry peers by +26 pp during the first stage of the COVID-19 pandemic.

**Transformations that increase operational flexibility boost adaptivity.** To succeed in crises—particularly during the recovery period, which can be unpredictable in timing and magnitude—companies need to rapidly adapt to the changing environment and scale up new models. Companies with greater operational flexibility (which we capture using the proxy of lower fixed asset intensity) can more easily adapt to outperforming during the recovery stage.

Companies with lower levels of asset ownership tend to have a higher proportion of variable costs, affording them the flexibility to tie costs closely to revenue in a downturn. They also tend to be less reliant on legacy assets, which creates an advantage in adapting to technological advances and seizing new market opportunities during the recovery. Our research shows that growth transformations that reduce fixed-asset intensity increase performance relative to industry during future market recoveries by +3 pp on average, whereas those that increase levels of fixed-asset ownership see no change in performance during the recovery stage.

From 2004 to 2006, consumer conglomerate Cendant Corporation undertook a strategic realignment to exit non core business segments with high levels of fixed assets. Over the two-year transformation, the organization initiated public offerings and spun off segments in tax services, real estate services, and fleet leasing—reducing fixed-asset intensity from 35% to 9% in the process.

Renaming the firm Avis Budget Group, the organization refocused its efforts on its core vehicle rental operations. With vehicles acquired under repurchase agreements (that allow for return of vehicles to manufacturer at set monthly depreciated value), the company now benefits from a highly variable cost structure. With the ability to quickly defleet during a downturn—and scale up during recovery—Avis was well-positioned when the global financial crisis hit. One year past the initial shock from the global financial crisis, Avis was +62 pp above preshock levels, while industry peers had yet to fully recover.

Taken together, transformations that accelerate growth, reduce debt loads, and increase operational flexibility improve performance relative to industry peers by +10 pp in response to future crises (Figure 4).

Mean change in industry-adjusted TSR in response to crises[1]

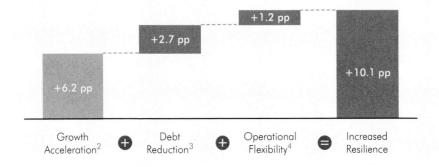

| Growth Acceleration[2] | ⊕ | Debt Reduction[3] | ⊕ | Operational Flexibility[4] | ⊜ | Increased Resilience |

1. Crisis quarter if peak decline in industry TSR exceeds 15 pp. Compares performance in response to industry shocks during 5-year periods preceding and following corporate transformation.
2. Growth acceleration if trailing 12-month growth in full-year following end of transformation is greater than trailing 12-month growth at start of transformation; deceleration otherwise.
3. Debt reduction defined as lower debt-EV ratio following transformation.
4. Increased operational flexibility defined as lower fixed asset intensity (net PPE/sales) following transformation.

**Figure 4.** Debt reduction and operational flexibility further improve resilience by 4 percentage points.

Source: S&P Capital IQ; BCG Henderson Institute analysis

## Don't Overlook Resilience in Good Times

The playbook for resilient transformations differs in a few fundamental ways from those that primarily aim to increase efficiency and optimize short-run financial performance. Transforming for resilience requires a new mindset, which unfortunately tends to fade as stability and prosperity return.

When a crisis is fresh, our research indicates that leaders are more likely to adopt an approach to transformation that is consistent with building resilience. Immediately following a crisis, transformations are 19% more likely to be growth oriented and 20% less likely to increase debt than those at least 12 months removed from a shock.

Put simply—as crisis fades from memory, leaders tend to neglect the importance of building resilience. Corporate change efforts tend to return to targeting cost reduction, stabilized corporate bond markets make debt financing more palatable, and the superior operational control afforded by asset ownership begins to look more attractive. Critically, however, the *value* of a resilient transformation remains the same—no matter the timing.

Future-oriented leaders recognize the long-term value of resilience and keep it on the change agenda in fair-weather times. Based on our proprietary natural language processing analysis of U.S. Securities and Exchange Commission filings and annual reports, we find that transformations accompanied by a long-term strategic orientation are 10% more likely to accelerate growth, 30% more likely to reduce debt, and 24% more likely to reduce fixed-asset ownership. For future-oriented leaders, keeping resilience on the transformation agenda pays off. Transformations that accelerate growth, reduce debt, and increase operational flexibility in *more stable periods* improve resilience by +7 pp more than those that do not.

## The Resilient Transformation Agenda

The COVID-19 pandemic and the Ukrainian war have brought the value of corporate resilience into focus, with many leaders now seeking to rebuild their organizations to be more resilient. The possibility of a recession may provide a third impetus to emphasize resilience. While every transformation is unique, our findings point toward a pattern of moves that can improve the odds of a resilient transformation:

1. **Transform with an opportunity mindset.** Defensive, cost-cutting measures might produce short-term gains, but fail to advance resilience in the long run. To build resilience—especially in the recovery stage of a crisis—corporate transformations must increase the organizational capacity for innovation and reinvention.
   *Imagination lies upstream of innovation.* Upstream of innovation lies imagination, the ability to conceive novelty in the world before attempting to produce it. Transformations that prioritize growth are those that increase the organizational ability to think counterfactually, break existing mental models, and conceive of the new ideas fitting for new environments. As such, transformations that push organizations to compete on imagination will be those best positioned to thrive in altered circumstances after the next crisis.

2. **Accelerate digital transformation.** Digital transformations, executed correctly, can improve resilience by increasing operational flexibility and positioning the firm to capture new growth opportunities. Digital transformation can increase operational flexibility and adaptivity—both critical capabilities in improving recovery speeds in future. Some asset-light companies take this approach even further by organizing in massive

digital ecosystems, effectively reducing asset intensity, pooling resources, spreading risk, and accelerating the scaling of new models and offerings. Companies that build a digital technology advantage *and* strategically deploy it can further benefit by extending the perceptive power of the organization to identify emergent opportunities. Digital transformations can also free up human cognition to focus on higher-level activities, such as imagination, to conceive of new ideas and identify fresh sources of growth. In doing so, they create significant advantage in the final stages of future crises as organizations reinvent themselves to succeed in the new post shock reality.

3. **Keep resilience on the transformation agenda in good times as well.** To capture the long-term competitive benefit of resilience in a very dynamic business environment, companies must transform with resilience in mind in stable times too.

Future crises are inevitable. Companies that recognize resilience as a long-term strategic imperative and make it a pillar of corporate change will be those best-positioned to outperform in future crises. As corporations ready themselves for reopening and growth, resilience is now at risk of losing the limelight. Change programs that prioritize growth over cost cutting, debt reduction over debt financing, and operational flexibility over direct control, will realize the full value of resilience and build advantage for the next crisis.

## About the Author

**Martin Roovoc** is Managing Director and Senior Partner in BCG's San Francisco office and Chairman of the BCG Henderson Institute, BCG's vehicle for exploring ideas from beyond the world of business, which have implications for business strategy management.

He is the coauthor of *The Imagination Machine* (HBR Press, 2021), *Your Strategy Needs a Strategy* (HBR Press, 2015), and the *Inspiring the Next Game* series (DeGruyter, 2021).

Martin joined BCG in London in 1989 and later moved to Tokyo, where he was responsible for BCG's business with Western clients. His consulting career has focused on strategy—with equal emphasis on idea origination and development, and application by consulting with clients on their strategy challenges. Martin holds a triple first-class MA in natural sciences from Cambridge University and an MBA from Cranfield School of Management.

# Resilience@Scale

GABRIELE ROSANI AND PAOLO CERVINI

19

Over the last two years, the COVID-19 pandemic has put immense pressure on governments and businesses around the world. Organizations have responded to this challenge by launching ambitious recovery and resilience initiatives to bounce back stronger in the new normal. Take, for example, the Recovery and Resilience Facility (RRF) at the heart of NextGenerationEU to help the European Union (EU) emerge stronger and more resilient from the current crisis. On the business side, companies have started transformative initiatives to adapt to a deeply changed context; consider, for instance, the massive shift determined by the hybrid work mode.

While we were coping with these challenges, another unanticipated crisis disrupted the recovery plans of most firms: the war in Ukraine made all forecasts obsolete in a matter of days.

While it's true that events of such magnitude (a global pandemic, a war in Europe) may be seen as exceptional occurrences, it's also true that in today's age of perpetual transformation, uncertainty and volatility are becoming the norm, not the exception in most sectors. It's not surprising then that resilience has risen to the top of many leaders' agendas. However, few companies have made resilience an organizational capability, baked into their routines and practices.

If uncertainty becomes a stable and permanent condition, organizations need to make resilience an enduring, pervasive, and continuous organizational practice (not just an occasional response to an extraordinary event). We call this type of resilience *resilience@scale*, as companies need to build a widespread capability to cope and thrive in a world of perpetual transformation.

The challenge is how to make resilience a practice adopted systematically by all functions and units regardless of where they are in the organization. Based on our research and hands-on experience with large companies, we have developed guiding principles and concrete tools for developing resilience@scale.

There are **four main principles** we recommend to follow when scaling a resilience practice into the whole organization:

1. **Decentralization:** While a major disruption with a global impact already gets full attention of the top-executive team, there are many (albeit smaller in magnitude) local crises from which the organization can learn and evolve. For example, reacting to duties imposed overnight in a developing country; adapting to supply chain disruption at a local harbor; an accident at a plant; a new local law or regulation; a market

scandal; a dramatic drop in sales due to customer default; data security breach; natural disaster; and so forth. On several occasions, those local disruptions are solved with creativity and fast actions put in place by a local team reacting to a crisis. In these events, there is much to learn once the emergency ends. However, in most organizations there's no structured practice or routine to extract all of the positives from unexpected events happening at the periphery of the organization. Not capturing and sharing these learnings systematically is a loss for the entire organization and should be avoided.

2. **Pervasiveness:** Capturing and sharing the learnings after a critical occurrence should not be limited to specific functions such as risk management. All functions and departments should exercise resilience thinking after every significant event happening in their domain—from sales and marketing to production and supply chain, from communications to HR; and in all geographies, not only central headquarters. Although the value of a single learning from one local event in one particular department may seem small or too specific, if you combine at scale all functions and all geographies, the sum of all parts is not trivial and can be compared to a larger event impacting the whole company.

3. **Endurance:** Resilience should be a continuous activity, not a once-in-a-decade reflection. In a context of perpetual transformation, resilience should be perpetual as well or at least having a periodical cadence (e.g., quarterly or yearly). Only if the reflection is conducted with frequency, can it become routine and get embedded in the operating models. The fact that the pandemic forced many organizations to pay attention to resilience creates a momentum for instilling a more systematic approach. On the contrary, if in one or two years from now the word *resilience* falls into oblivion, companies will have missed a huge opportunity to build a competitive advantage around it.

4. **Curation:** Decentralization, pervasiveness, and endurance require a well-orchestrated coordination process to make sure that a reflection on resilience is part of the way of working in all functions and geographies. Imagine a process that collects input periodically from the edges of the organization into a sort of central engine, capable of consolidating all of the learnings so they are available and searchable. Consider the

following case: When a supply chain manager in Taiwan faces a local disruption related to local harbor blockage, they can search for similar events that happened elsewhere in the company and take insights and ideas for solutions rather than having to invent them firsthand.

These four principles can guide a firm designing a resilience@scale system. In more concrete terms, there are a couple of simple tools that could be easily adopted to start the practice and instill a routine. We have witnessed the effectiveness of these tools in different departments, from HR to operations.

The first tool is called *resilience retrospective*; it draws an analogy from the practice, common in agile approaches to project management, for teams to meet one hour or so at a specific cadence to discuss what went well and what needs improvement for the next cycle. What does a resilience retrospective look like? In a specific department, select members of the local team join together to reflect about the crisis events that may have occurred in the past quarters and the way those events were tackled and solved: what was positive, what created challenges, and how to deal with those circumstances next time. As an output of this retrospective session, the team summarizes the main learnings in terms of concrete ideas for radical or incremental improvement.

For example, within the HR department of a large utility company, the subteam in charge of new hire onboarding faced challenges in the first months of the pandemic, as most employees had to work remotely. They had to quickly come up with concrete ideas on how to adjust the onboarding process to fit the new conditions. They exercised a lot of creativity, regardless of the standard procedures, to make sure that new hires would feel welcomed and rapidly integrated into the company despite the constraints.

This was originally meant as a temporary measure to deal with the crisis. However, when the pandemic eased and restrictions were removed, the team decided to run a resilience retrospective to critically review which ideas could be leveraged and maintained in the new normal: rather than bouncing back to the original process, they bounced forward by embracing some of the changes as permanent solutions. Several in-presence bureaucratic fulfillments previously mandatory now can be arranged remotely for a smoother digital experience. The results of the retrospective (see Table 1) were shared with other HR departments in other countries. The best practices at the local level were considered by the global function when redesigning the onboarding

**Table 1.** Illustrative Example of a Resilience Retrospective in the HR Department of a Large Utility

| Scope of the Retrospective | |
|---|---|
| Examples of areas to consider in the retrospection reflection: employee journey, digital/physical mix; interactions, administrative burden, flexibility… | |
| **What works well** | **What can be improved** |
| Signs and sends the contract digitally<br><br>Receives the (digital) onboarding diary | Receives welcome kit at home 1 week prior to first official day<br><br>Orders any assets for remote working from the catalog<br><br>Receives a welcome video or message from their team |

procedures for the new normal (the procedure that is now in place). Although this was an experiment, the team sees value in establishing the resilience retrospective as routine on a periodic basis.

Let's look at another example in a different department: the plant operations of a large oil and gas company (this example is not related to the COVID-19 pandemic and shows that the approach can work in all critical events). One of the company's plants in southern Europe had a fire (luckily without casualties for the operators, thanks to a prompt intervention). The local department organized a resilience retrospective session to reflect on the incident and derive learnings on what to change in the procedures to reduce the risk of a new event. They shared the results of the session in a meeting with other European company plants.

The second tool for resilience in practice is what we call the Resilience Matrix (see an illustrative example in Table 2), a summary map of the various resilience retrospectives used in the different departments and countries of the company and consolidated into a visual frame. The matrix represents a curated review of the main learnings, and ideas emerged during the resilience cycle of the year (or half year). This can be done at multiple levels: country, regional, and global with varying degrees of granularity and aggregation and discussed by the appropriate line of management.

**Table 2.** Illustrative Example of a Resilience Matrix

| Resilience Matrix — Region X, year YY | Event Type | Root Causes | Lessons Learned |
|---|---|---|---|
| HR | Kidnapping of a worker and ransom request. | Security measures were not increased despite country's higher risk. | Rethink frequency of assessment and continuous updating. |
| Operations | Shut down for one week due to critical failure in electrical equipment. | Maintenance contract was not flexible enough to ensure a quick fix.<br><br>Poor service. | Change service provider.<br><br>Change contractual rules. |
| Supply Chain | Sanctions on a country that is a major supplier of a key component. | Overexposure to one supplier; no redundancy. | Revise criteria for sourcing, introducing resilience. |
| Health, Safety, and Environment | Fire in the plant. | Some operators did not know (or did not follow) the safety practices. | More training on how to use equipment. |
| Sales and Marketing | A main customer has a cash liquidity crisis. | Accommodating payment terms was difficult due to the inflexibility of global procedures. | Provide flexibility to the local team under certain conditions. |
| Communications | Social media storm about a recent advertisement. | Not issuing an immediate statement was a mistake.<br><br>The advertisement should have been removed immediately. | Include this recommendation in the communication guidelines. |

Single functions (on the rows of the matrix) first conduct their own reflections to discuss their specific events and learnings. Such a retrospective can occur during the quarterly or yearly review meetings of the function's management. The consolidation of all functions is then discussed at the global or regional level during periodic business unit reviews, where all functional leaders of the unit are present. The cross-functionality is important to de-silo discussions and foster a more holistic view of the interdependencies of resilience (for example, a supply chain issue because of an operator strike in a plant due to safety concerns).

Having discussions on resilience on the agenda of business review meetings is a good practice, which increases awareness and helps instill a new mindset in the management team. It signals that resilience is as relevant as other core elements of the business and should not be relegated to the corner of the risk management department. The output of the discussions and the commented matrix can be shared and cascaded more broadly and transparently within the organization, for example, making it accessible and visible in the intranet rather than keeping it hidden in a drawer. This will reinforce a culture of learning from mistakes, fostering psychological safety at all levels of the organization.

History tells us that companies often lose interest in resilience as crises fade. They see resilience as an exception. If this might have been okay in previous decades, in the last few years we have witnessed a series of unprecedented political, societal, economic, technological, and environmental changes with transformational impacts on markets and businesses.

To cope with a world in perpetual transformation, companies need to embed resilience as a routine baked into the organization rather than an exception handled by a few experts.

Seeing resilience as a pervasive and decentralized practice can yield significant benefits for the organization in term of creativity, adaptability, flexibility, and quick responses to the challenges various functions and areas of the company may face.

Resilience@scale should be everybody's job—a capability at scale across the entire organization (functions, countries, business units). Simple tools and practices, such as the resilience retrospective and the resilience matrix, can help and should be institutionalized as a routine.

## About the Authors

**Gabriele Rosani** is Director of Content & Research at Capgemini Invent's Management Lab. His contributions are featured in leading management magazines, including HBR.org, *The European Business Review, Dialogue Review*, and *I by IMD*.

**Paolo Cervini** is Vice President and Co-lead of Capgemini Invent's Management Lab.

Prior to joining CapGemini, Gabriele and Paolo were part of the leadership team of ECSI (European Centre for Strategic Innovation), a management research and innovation consultancy.

# Beyond Resilience: Leaders Must Urgently Embrace Antifragility

RICARDO VIANA VARGAS

# 20

In 1968, the government of Manitoba—a medium-sized province located at the geographic center of Canada—completed what was, at that time, one of the great engineering marvels of the developed world: the Red River Floodway. The floodway is a 47-kilometer-long earthen channel used to divert surging water from the notoriously flood-prone Red River around the city of Winnipeg (Manitoba's capital). The idea for the channel was first proposed by a government commission following the devastating flood of 1950 that completely submerged Winnipeg, requiring more than 100,000 people to be evacuated and causing damage that would amount to, in 2022 dollars, more than CA$11 billion. Even though the benefits were many, most political leaders shied away from the project. Most, but not all.

Dufferin "Duff" Roblin, leader of the Progressive Conservative Party of Manitoba, was perhaps the biggest fan of the floodway concept. After winning the 1958 election and forming the local government, Roblin set to work getting funding from the federal government to build the floodway. Started in 1962, it would take six years to complete and required 76 million cubic meters of earth—equivalent to 30,000 Olympic-sized swimming pools—to be excavated and moved. That made the floodway, at the time, the second-largest earth-moving project in the world after the Panama Canal.

And yet, both before breaking ground and throughout the project, Roblin was assailed for spending tens of millions of dollars on something so ambitious. Critics nicknamed the project "Roblin's Folly" and suggested it would ruin the provincial treasury.

Roblin not only endured in the face of such criticism, he pushed on and finished the project. He had lived through the devastation of the 1950 flood and was not going to allow that kind of disaster to occur ever again. Roblin was prescient in this commitment; since it was completed, it is estimated the floodway has been used to save the capital city of Winnipeg from being inundated by the murky waters of the Red River nearly two dozen times, preventing more than CA$10 billion in damages.

Roblin, and the floodway that is now known more affectionately as "Duff's Ditch," is not only a great example of the limitless possibilities of engineering, it is a fascinating study of leadership. Not only did Roblin withstand the political and public oppositions to his plan to build the floodway, he seemed encouraged by it and pushed through to complete a project that certainly would have died on the drawing table without his efforts.

Interestingly, Roblin is often cited as an example of resilient leadership, although that term—resilient—doesn't quite capture the magnitude or the true nature of what he did. He did not just endure, he seemed to gain energy with each naysayer and protest.

No, Roblin was not an example of a resilient leader; he was the antifragile leader.

## Antifragile Leadership in an Age of Constant Crisis Management

The concept of antifragility was developed by Nassim Taleb, a noted Lebanese-American author, mathematician, and risk analyst. In his best-selling 2012 book, *Antifragile: Things that Gain from Disorder*, Taleb argues that antifragility is a response that some people experience when they are faced with a threat or a sudden shock. "Some things benefit from shocks; they thrive and grow when exposed to volatility, randomness, disorder, and stressors and love adventure, risk, and uncertainty," Taleb writes in the prologue. "Yet, in spite of the ubiquity of the phenomenon, there is no word for the exact opposite of fragile. Let us call it antifragile. Antifragility is beyond resilience or robustness. The resilient resists shocks and stays the same; the antifragile gets better" (Taleb, 2012, p. 3).

Why is it important to expand our definition of resilient leadership, particularly when it is in such fashion today? A quick visit to Google's search engine with the terms "resilient" and "leadership" reveal that, within the confines of the leadership development industry, a large and pervasive cottage industry has settled on imparting best practices to build resilience. However, as Taleb notes in his thesis, the ability to endure or withstand the conditions that come with a crisis or disaster is simply not enough; leaders must show a capacity to learn from each crisis and evolve.

There is a consensus building among academics, researchers, and psychologists that the need to simultaneously trying to juggle multiple crises and disasters—climate change, public health threats, economic uncertainty and, most recently, war on a scale not seen in decades—is moving the leadership development needle away from resilience to antifragility. The COVID-19 pandemic in particular provides multiple examples of both antifragile and fragile leadership in action.

When the pandemic first struck in early 2020, virtually no country on Earth was fully prepared. Not that they weren't warned.

Going as far back as 2014, luminaries, such as Microsoft founder Bill Gates, were pleading with nations and corporate interests alike to start building the infrastructure to contain and combat something like COVID-19. He told the world that a pandemic like the one we are experiencing now could be more devastating to the world than a nuclear war.

As he watches the world struggle with the coronavirus, it would be easy for Gates to shrug his shoulders with an "I-told-you-so" indifference and point fingers at everyone who ignored his warnings. Instead, Gates is accepting some of the blame, arguably for not taken a more antifragile approach to this existential threat. "I feel terrible," Gates told *The Wall Street Journal* in May 2020. "The whole point of talking about (a pandemic) was that we could take action and minimize the damage."

Once the pandemic hit, the line between fragile and antifragile leadership became even more pronounced. In countries such as the United States and the United Kingdom, the pandemic response strategy blended equal measures of panic and politics. State leaders could not separate personal or political ideology from science and common sense. The result was not just a level of chaos that seemed incongruent with the otherwise evolved nature of their countries, but also a loss of life that far exceeded anyone's expectation.

There were also examples of true antifragile leadership in action, none as powerful as New Zealand Prime Minister Jacinda Ardern. Faced with a growing public health threat and virtually no national pandemic infrastructure, Ardern was among the first political leaders to show the resolve to impose severe social and economic restrictions and close her country's borders after the virus first appeared. New Zealand became one of the first countries to introduce a pandemic alert system to guide decisions on social and economic restrictions. She established an all-star panel of scientific and medical experts who not only helped guide government policy and strategy, but also publicly critiqued government performance.

Her recipe for success involved clear empathy for the plight of her citizens, highly visible leadership—she appeared on some platform almost every day—and firm, science-based public health decisions. Ardern did not just demonstrate resilience in the face of this crisis, she learned from it in real time, applied those lessons, put aside personal values, listened to her experts, and maintained an open dialogue with her citizens.

Ardern is certainly a model of how leaders must do more than just stand firm in the face of a crisis. They must find ways of learning from the crisis and introduce more robust measures in response. But is her combination of empathy and firm decision-making something other leaders can emulate?

**Building Antifragile Leaders**

Experts in the fields of project management and emergency management have always preached the importance of being decisive, responsive, and accountable to both the people they lead, and the ultimate goal which, when facing a crisis, has to be learning and evolving in ways that our responses become more effective and robust. However, to build a culture of antifragile leadership, organizations need to be able to identify and impart certain core capacities to their leaders.

But where to start? Many parallels have been drawn between the VUCA model of leadership and antifragility. VUCA is an acronym that stands for volatility, uncertainty, complexity, and ambiguity. Created by leadership scholars Warren Bennis and Burt Nanus in the late 1980s, VUCA has been adopted and absorbed into many streams of leadership development, including the U.S. Armed Forces, which applies it in several areas of curricula at its educational centers. Although VUCA is a way of defining the qualities of a crisis, it also preaches the importance of leaders developing the capacity to respond to all four pillars and develop more robust responses.

The qualities of antifragile leadership can be described in many different ways. However, when you boil down all of the semantic variations, you come up with some common themes.

**Antifragile leaders are accountable.** In *The Leadership Contract*, leadership advisor and consultant Dr. Vince Molinaro sets out a number of conditions that allow leaders to more effective in today's dynamic environment. He notes that leaders must be deliberate in their decisions to take on a leadership role (Molinaro, 2017). There can be no equivocation about taking on the mantle of leadership; uncertainty or ambivalence are not positive leadership qualities. However, he also notes that once you have truly committed to being a leader, you must also acknowledge your obligations, particularly the reality that you will be held to higher standards and be expected to put in a lot of hard work to live up to those standards. Finally, he argues that to be truly accountable and effective, leaders must have access to a community of peers to gain support and insight into their day-to-day challenges. Taken together, these four pillars form a contract that all leaders must commit to living each and every day.

**Although decisive, antifragile leaders score high on emotional intelligence.** It would be easy to conflate antifragile leadership with traditional, top-down, command-and-control style leadership, where there is no time to consult, confer, or seek consensus on decisions. In some instances, it may even be considered impossible to communicate the reasons behind decisions. However, experts in the field of crisis management know that communication, consultation, and empathy are important qualities in delivering an effective response. This is consistent with many of the precepts in Taleb's original thinking on antifragility: leaders can never seek to build their own antifragility at the expense of others' fragility. Other leading thinkers in this discipline believe it is essential leaders apply best practices in psychological trauma intervention to help build support and confidence. What connects these concepts is that a crisis is essentially an emotional experience; leaders must be able to demonstrate emotional intelligence to truly achieve a state of antifragility.

**Antifragile leaders understand that it is never too late to prepare for a worst-case scenario.** As was the case in our initial anecdote about flood-channel champion Duff Roblin, antifragile leaders have the courage to prepare for a crisis rather than just scramble to respond once one appears. A good example can be found at the All-England Lawn Tennis Association, the group that hosts the Wimbledon tennis tournament. Shortly after the pandemic struck in 2020, and professional sporting events were canceled all over the world, it was learned that the All-England Lawn Tennis Association had, for the past two decades, purchased pandemic insurance. At a cost of US$1.9 million annually, this was no small decision by leaders at the tournament. However, once it was learned the policy would pay out US$141 million to compensate organizers for the cancellation of the 2020 tournament, the prescient wisdom of their decision became clear. The All-England club demonstrated antifragile leadership through its bold and courageous decision to protect its marquee event from disruption caused by a public health emergency.

Antifragile leaders do not dwell on failure; they shift focus immediately to solutions. The disciples of antifragile leadership love a good anecdote about organizations that are able to somehow snatch victory from the jaws of what appears to be certain defeat. One of the most referenced stories is the comeback by the Toyota Motor Corporation. From 2009 to 2011, in the wake of the global financial crisis, Toyota was rocked by a series of recalls that affected tens of millions of cars worldwide, some of which had been involved in fatal accidents owing to vehicle malfunctions. Its share prices tumbled, and losses exceeded an astronomical US$21 billion. However, the company launched an ambitious recovery plan under the leadership of President Akio Toyoda, the grandson of the company's founder. Using a combination of aggressive marketing and ruthless dedication to quality control, Toyota rebounded: by 2015, the company's profits grew to a record US$18 billion, up nearly 20% from the previous year.

## Conclusion

The challenge in leadership development, particularly as it applies to crisis management, is to find a way of changing organizational culture rather than individual behavior. All of the great antifragile leaders we have discussed worked first to create the conditions necessary for antifragility to take hold. In other words, nobody can force someone to learn and grow from adversity. The logic of antifragility needs to be embedded in an organization's leadership culture so that it takes root and grows.

## References

Molinaro, V. (2017). *The leadership contract* (3rd ed.). Wiley.

Taleb, N. (2012). *Antifragile: Things that gain from disorder*. Random House.

## About the Author

Passionate about transforming ideas into action, **Ricardo Vargas** is a chief advocate in the project economy. Specializing in implementing innovative global initiatives, capital projects, and product development, Ricardo has directed dozens of projects across industries and continents, managing more than US$20 billion in global initiatives over the past 25 years.

Ricardo shares his expertise with millions of professionals around the globe through his "5 Minutes Podcast," which he has hosted since 2007. He has written 16 books on project management, risk and crisis management, and transformation, which have been translated into six languages and sold more than half a million copies. His influence on the sector was affirmed when he became the first Latin American to be elected Chairman of the Project Management Institute (PMI).

More than two decades ago, he founded Macrosolutions, a global consulting firm with international operations in energy, infrastructure, IT, oil, and finance. His work as a venture capitalist and entrepreneur in artificial intelligence, blockchain, big data, chatbots, and machine learning resulted in tools and products that have revolutionized how users bring agility and agile management into project management software.

Between 2016 and 2020, Ricardo directed the Brightline® Initiative, a Project Management Institute think tank bringing together leading organizations into a coalition dedicated to helping executives bridge the expensive, unproductive gap between strategic design and delivery. Prior to his work with Brightline®, Ricardo was Director of the United Nations Office for Project Services (UNOPS) Infrastructure and Project Management Group, leading more than 1,000 projects and US$1.2 billion in humanitarian and development projects.

Ricardo holds a PhD in civil engineering from Federal Fluminense University in Brazil and an undergraduate degree in chemical engineering, as well as a master's degree in industrial engineering from Federal University of Minas Gerais in Brazil.

# Resilience Drives Strategy Execution

FLEMMING VIDERIKSEN AND PARISA LOUIE

**21**

Today crises are the norm, not the exception. Companies need intelligent strategic thinking to build sufficient resilience to withstand the waves of change washing over them. With a clear line of sight and a sharp distinction between business operations and business change, you can exploit momentum and create opportunities out of crises. Technology can also help engage the whole organization in doing the right things at the right time.

We live in a world where crises and change are inevitable. Disasters come more often and their impact on society seems to be escalating. Think pandemics, climate change, war, terrorism, financial crises, embargoes, volatile energy prices, and shortages of food and other resources. These major disruptions lead to conflicts within countries, companies, and organizations, as well as at a personal level. Our theory is that instead of preventing crises, which is impossible, we need to make ourselves robust. We need, as the saying goes, to build resilience.

Employees need to be resilient to avoid the stress of increased workload or organizational change. Cities must be resilient when faced with extreme weather events. Businesses need to be resilient to cope with changing competitive conditions, labor shortages, and unforeseen regulations. If you are resilient, you can come through a crisis unscathed and, eventually, even come out stronger on the other side.

## No Resilience Without Strategy

Some argue that a changeable world calls for adaptability rather than plans and strategies. We believe that it makes no sense to talk about resilience without talking about strategy and vice versa; the two are symbiotic and now more so than ever before. The problem with traditional strategic thinking, especially execution, is that strategies die if they are overtaken by reality, which unfortunately happens in far too many companies and organizations. As General and later President Dwight D. Eisenhower supposedly once said: "plans are worthless, but planning is everything." (Eisenhower, 1950).

The solution is not less strategy, fewer values, and fewer long-term goals, but rather working toward those goals with a better ability to adapt strategy along the way. To be able to do this requires quick reactions, decisions based on real-time data, and, not the least, an ability to get everyone in the organization engaged in making the strategy happen.

In this article, we describe what happens to companies that are not resilient to change and how the best-performing organizations increase their resilience through intelligent strategic thinking. We also show that there is a link among resilience, successful strategy execution, and positive performance by firms. We examine areas, such as organizational culture, management processes, and tools for governance and reporting, and we describe how these influence successful strategy execution and resilience.

In the last part of the article, we also offer a proven method to make values, long-term goals, and resilience go hand in hand. It's not difficult. You just need to follow four simple steps to create an organizational culture of resilience that can make your strategies viable in an ever-changing world. You'll look at strategy implementation and execution with fresh eyes. So, here we go....

## Running the Business Versus Changing the Business

The core element of most organizations is their operations—all activities involved in running the business. If an organization's revenues are derived primarily from its products, its fundamental activities are supply, design, production, distribution, marketing, and sales. This concept is reflected in Porter's Value Chain. For the sake of simplicity, running the business can be divided into four main components:

- Shareholders
- Top management
- Core activities
- Supporting activities

The other dimension to running the business are a company's projects, the activities that change the business. Projects are restricted in terms of time and budget and are staffed with temporary team members; they need different types of resources. Project leaders must work to bring different views together, which requires diplomacy and negotiation skills. They must also be good at managing uncertainty, because large strategic projects are not predictable from one week to the next.

After a project is completed, the operations side takes over. For example, consider a technology company that decides to develop a new digital tablet. The project's estimated cost is €15 million (US$15.6 million), with expected revenues around €100 million (US$104 million). Once the tablet has been designed, the organization's operations side will take over. The marketing team will launch the product, and the sales team will sell the tablet and aim to achieve the target revenue of €100 million. It's often in the process between run and change where strategy is lost in implementation. Resilient strategy execution and rigid strategic governance will help make these transitions seamless and successful.

## Growth Versus Productivity-Related Projects

The most strategic projects have a robust external focus, with a goal that is related to revenue and profitability growth. In contrast, the least strategic projects are internally focused, with a goal that often involves productivity improvements, either via cost reduction or increased asset performance. When a company launches a new project, one of its main objectives must be to either increase growth or improve productivity and performance. The more strategic projects (growth related) are typically sponsored by the business and corporate departments, whereas the less strategic projects (productivity related) are launched by support functions.

Increasing a company's growth and profitability purely through operational changes is limited to a few strategic decisions: raising prices, reducing prices, producing more products or services, entering new markets, or introducing new products or versions. CEOs and senior management prefer more strategic initiatives because they produce the highest returns and the most significant benefits, including increased robustness and resilience. However, such initiatives are typically costlier, riskier, and deliver benefits that require more time to realize. And don't forget: to succeed, much of the organization—not just the project team—needs to be involved. That's not easy, but there's no alternative if a business is to thrive in an ever-changing reality.

## Companies Also Get Sick

Since the beginning of the COVID-19 pandemic in 2019—and most recently with the outbreak of the war in Ukraine in early 2022—major changes have turned the world upside down. COVID-19 cost human lives, but its effects on business have also been profound. Just as people get sick, so do companies. In the United States in 2020, 630 relatively large firms—defined as public companies with assets or liabilities of at least US$2 million or private companies with at least US$10 million of the same—went bankrupt (Irum & Hudgins, 2021). That was an increase of 9% from the year before and the highest level of annual bankruptcies for a decade.

In addition to death and destruction, the war in Ukraine led to massive falls in stock markets, and energy prices rocketing to levels not seen since the energy crisis of the 1970s. Food prices have risen accordingly, certain resources have become scarce, and businesses are experiencing a degree of unpredictability that makes it very difficult for them to navigate safely toward the desired end state. Both large and small organizations are at risk. In the United Kingdom, as gas prices rose, 31 energy firms ceased trading between the beginning of 2021 and February 2022 (Cyrus, 2022). Meanwhile, more than one-third of the country's iconic fish and chip shops could go out of business (Choudhry, 2022). Up to 40% of the United Kingdom's whitefish, such as cod and haddock, comes from Russia, which controls nearly 45% of the global supply. Ukraine is also the largest producer of the sunflower oil in which the fish is fried (Seafish.org, 2022).

In situations like this, it is not enough just to make a plan. It is equally important to execute that strategy properly and to monitor the process in as close to real time as possible. While in the past the way to do that might have been via nothing more sophisticated than a CEO's notebook, today there are technological tools that can assist. By using these tools, it is possible to find quick wins and long-term benefits and for businesses to gain a higher degree of overall resilience.

## Crisis as an Opportunity

It is important to use any crisis situation as an opportunity to build excellence in strategy execution and bring strategy to the core of the organization. Firms that can quickly execute and adjust strategies will have far better chances of survival and success.

As a report from management consultants Kearney summarized:
What the pandemic did for Uber, Ford, General Motors, the airlines, and dozens of other companies was let them redeploy physical assets by focusing on how they make things rather than exclusively on what they make. The true power of strategic deconstruction was tapped by moving past physical process into purpose-based activities. (Guerard & Portell, 2022).

The objective for a company when emerging from a crisis should not be just to get through it as smoothly as possible, but rather to come back stronger. It is easy, when the immediate emergency has passed, for an institution to drift. In Iceland, several businesses congratulated themselves on weathering the immediate economic downturn after the 2008 financial crisis—which took down Icelandic banks with total assets of US$155 billion—only to succumb to a slow decline over the longer period that followed.

By contrast, Reykjavik Energy (RE), the world's largest producer of geothermal energy, and likewise in crisis post-2008, was able to stay on track. RE initially developed a five-year plan that became the focus of everything that followed. It was simply called "THE PLAN;" everyone knew it and could relate to it. The company rebuilt the entire leadership team, worked to align core values with regular measurements, and gave all units of the organization ownership of the strategy. RE achieved all of the goals of the five-year plan within four years.

Similarly, Icelandic supermarket giant COOP (Samkaup) managed to include 1,400 employees in 60 stores across a large geographical area in contributing to their strategy. COOP involved managers and employees to unlock the company's growth potential. In four years, the supermarket chain went from the bottom position in employee satisfaction surveys to the very top. By executing a four-year people and culture strategy, the company has succeeded in making employees one of the most important competitive assets of the organization. At the same time, Samkaup has become a sought-after workplace, rewarded for its efforts in nurturing relationships with its employees.

## Strategy Execution Needs an Operational Back End

The introduction of new software tools takes time and effort. Business leaders are understandably sometimes wary of doing this. But, given the striking difference today in the tools and level of sophistication firms use to manage manufacturing and logistical processes compared with their strategy implementation, it is time to bring the latter up to speed. We should retire the CEO's notebook for good.

The problem—given the scale and complexity of modern organizations— is really one of monitoring. Today, enterprise resource planning (ERP) software provides CEOs and shareholders with real-time data on the financial underpinnings of a company. They can see everything, from cash flow to inventory levels.

When it comes to strategy, matters are often much more primitive. Spreadsheets or scribbled notes in a CEO's notebook are often the only monitoring machinery that exists. The problem is a failure to acknowledge that, as with any other business function, strategy requires an operational back end to monitor and implement, just as trading or procurement does. Otherwise, matters do not stay on track.

Examples of corporate strategies devised at great cost and then failed to be implemented properly are numerous. To give one example, in the 1960s and 1970s the Schlitz Brewing Company, one of American's most famous beer makers, aimed to increase the speed-to-market and profitability of its product (Cornell, 2010). However, the measures they took, first incrementally replacing barley malt with corn syrup—hoping that consumers would not notice as the changes took place, and later cutting brewing time—produced a beer that tasted appalling and was lined with sediment, comparable with mucus.

Some means for keeping strategy on track are structural. It is wise for businesses to establish strategic governance committees to oversee implementation in the same way that another committee might oversee capital expenditure. Likewise, the position of chief strategy officer (CSO) should be as standard as that of a chief financial officer (CFO) or chief operating officer (COO). As with staffing, choosing the right people and ensuring that the committee has sufficient power are crucial. Further down the corporate hierarchy, it's useful to reduce or eliminate job descriptions in pursuit of greater agility—this enables individuals to focus on outcomes (benefits) and not on processes.

There is also a role here for technology. There's an emerging market for software solutions that provide cloud-based, real-time dashboards for strategy execution management for firms of any size. These products let business leaders actually transform strategy into action. A simple interface shows progress toward specific, defined goals and indicates where problems have occurred. Such platforms are now standard ways to manage many business processes—from logistics to manufacturing—with much greater efficiency. The opportunity here is to experience the same gain with strategy

### Four Steps to Resilient Strategy Execution

If you can't afford to lose another strategy at the implementation stage, or if you want to build resilience to withstand the challenges of a fast-changing world, then it's time to take strategy execution seriously. Make it the core of your organization and implement modern tools to drive execution and follow-ups.

There is more than one way to implement your plan, but it is essential that you remain consistent: keep trying and, if necessary, fail fast, then reshape your approach. To succeed, you need a structured plan, a tangible set of goals, and instant and transparent follow-up. If you follow this four-step plan, you will be in the best position:

1. **Optimize your ability to execute strategy:** Make a strategy for your strategy execution to drive speed and agility. Define the ambition for your strategy execution. Define what successful strategy execution looks like in your organization and how to make it happen. Establish a clear end state to strive for and ensure everyone on the management team is aligned and committed to your strategy execution plan.

2. **Design an execution-ready strategy:** To create focus, make sure that your strategy can be executed when you design it. Decide on a strategic framework. Assess the internal strength of the organization through an examination of the whole organization to determine its state of health and to identify potential improvement points. Establish your strategic hierarchy.

3. **Engage the entire organization:** To drive alignment and execution, secure a clear line of sight and establish an understanding of how to engage the organization. Prepare leadership for horizontal and vertical strategic alignment and buy-in to secure the engagement of employees to actively support and participate in your plan. Empower people to act independently on mutual goals, involve your people in the dialogue, and help them understand your strategy and how they can contribute to its success.

4. **Take strategic governance seriously:** Deploy strategic infrastructure to drive governance and accountability. Establish the same rigor in governing your strategy as you do for your finances. Make implementation a top priority to build trust and engagement throughout the organization. Use digital tools to access any element of strategy implementation at any time; because transparency, clear accountability, frequent reviews, and swift adjustments drive the execution of the strategy. Delegate responsibility and promptly resolve any deviations from the stated plan.

## References

Choudhry, S. (2022). Food shortages could force 'a third' of fish and chips shops to close. *Sky News.* May 15. https://news.sky.com/story/food-shortages-could-force-a-third-of-fish-and-chips-shops-to-close-12613442

Cornell, M. (2010). How Milwaukee's famous beer became infamous. *Beer Connoisseur.* October 1. https://beerconnoisseur.com/articles/how-milwaukees-famous-beer-became-infamous

Cyrus, C. (2022). Failed UK energy suppliers update. *Forbes Advisor.* February 18. https://www.forbes.com/uk/advisor/energy/failed-uk-energy-suppliers-update/

Eisenhower, D. (1950). https://quoteinvestigator.com/2017/11/18/planning/

Guerard, L. & Portell, G. (2022). *Deconstructing the building blocks of strategy.* A. T. Kearney. https://www.kearney.com/consumer-retail/article/-/insights/deconstructing-the-building-blocks-of-strategy

Irum, T. & Hudgins, C. (2021). *US corporate bankruptcies end 2020 at 10-year high amid COVID-19 pandemic.* S&P Global Market Intelligence. January 5. https://www.spglobal.com/marketintelligence/en/news-insights/latest-news-headlines/us-corporate-bankruptcies-end-2020-at-10-year-high-amid-covid-19-pandemic-61973656

Seafish.org. (2022). *Russian invasion of Ukraine: Implications for the UK seafood supply chain.* March 11. https://www.seafish.org/about-us/news-blogs/russian-invasion-of-ukraine-implications-for-the-uk-seafood-supply-chain/

## About the Authors

**Flemming Videriksen** and **Parisa Louie** are cofounders of DecideAct.